To
Mr Alvin Thaler
with best wishes
Hill Shine
Helen Shine

December
1949

The Quarterly Review
Under Gifford

The Quarterly Review Under Gifford

IDENTIFICATION OF CONTRIBUTORS
1809-1824

by

HILL SHINE

and

HELEN CHADWICK SHINE

THE UNIVERSITY OF NORTH CAROLINA PRESS
Chapel Hill · 1949

To

Sir John Murray

50 Albemarle Street

Publisher, Editor, Scholar
and kindly patron of scholars

INTRODUCTION

Seven years ago, when we began thinking of a history of the early *Quarterly Review,* we were confronted by the difficult problems of authorship. Obviously many different men's views had been fused, or mixed, to make up *The Quarterly* under Gifford. Some of the contributors were giants, and some were lesser men. But *who* had written *what* through that period had not been adequately dealt with anywhere. While a great many of the authorships had been identified in one place or another, some had been conflictingly reported by various students of the question. Some students had presented the evidence for their conclusions; some none. And many of the authorships had not been indicated at all. All the published data needed to be put together in one place; and all unpublished materials that could be gathered needed to be brought to bear along with it. So, with a clear and necessary problem in mind, we proceeded. One of us, a fast reader, undertook to work through the published memoirs and letters of likely persons. The other undertook analyses of the periodical articles themselves. Thus with daily comments on what we had found, the collection of materials for a history of the early *Quarterly* proceeded satisfactorily. But during the last two years, since the manuscript materials have been available, that division of labor has been suspended; and this first volume, on authorship, has required the time of both. Now that it is finished and its results are in usable form, we shall go on together in the preparation of the history. We hope that the future stages will prove as interesting as the past. If our work thus far has been agreeable, much of our gratitude is due to scholars like Graham, Clark, Brightfield, and Grierson, who have worked there before us.

In our description of the 733 *Quarterly* articles published during Gifford's editorship, we use three terms of classification. (1) The term *identified* means that some manuscript or printed source has indicated the identity of the reviewer(s), and that we have discovered no conflicting external evidence of equal or higher authority to discount the attribution. (2) The phrase *tentatively identified* means that, although some manuscript or printed source has implied the identity of the reviewer, the imputing source itself may have admitted uncertainty; or, as is frequently the case, some additional circumstantial evidence has made that attribution seem questionable or doubtful. A question mark placed before the name of an author in the text is the sign of this second classification. And (3) the phrase *totally unidentified* means that we have found no valid documentary evidence, in manuscript or in print external to the article itself, attributing that article to any particular writer. Thus of the 733 articles published under Gifford, 616 are identified; 60 are tentatively identified; and 57 are totally unidentified. Of the total 616 identifications, slightly more than a third (212) are now reported for the first time; they are based upon manuscript source materials.

At many times in the preparation of this volume, there has been need for careful judgment. No doubt mistakes have been made. But in every entry, we have taken pains to provide, so far as lay in our power, the means for correcting possible error. That is, we have provided in each entry a full record of the external documentary evidence that we have used. The temptation to call in the stylistic evidence—as without doubt a number of our documentary sources have in some degree called it into count—has perhaps been greatest in the smallest class referred to above: the class including fifty-seven totally unidentified articles. Special ones of these fifty-seven pieces strongly suggest the handiwork of Barrow, of Croker, or of Gifford. For that reason, such articles might have seemed easy to move over into the tentatively identified classification. But their presence in that new class would not have remained simple. Indeed, the procedure of presenting the mixed evidence, documentary *and* stylistic, would have become too complicated to be effective. And the consequent necessity of reducing stylistic evidence to intelligible symbols would have defeated our purpose of recording all the evidence upon which our judgments are based. Therefore in this volume we have deliberately limited ourselves to the external documentary evidence bearing upon authorship. On that sort of foundation, some solid assurance can be built up, step by step, in the rather slippery field of early 19th-century periodical literature. In the History, which is to come, the stylistic evidence, along with the other, will have its proper hearing.

Before we go into particular attributions in our text, a rapid and general glance at *The Quarterly's* contents and contributors should be interesting. First of all, one notices the wide variety of subjects. They range from theology to children's books, from philosophy to folklore. There are articles on mathematics, astronomy, and physics; medicine and surgery; chemistry, geology, and agriculture. There are accounts of politics and education in Britain, alongside of accounts of antipodal tribes and cultures, Arctic as well as tropical explorations, and excavations in the Egypt of the Pharaohs. There is history, from the ancient world to the modern. There are discussions of military forces and strategy, naval tactics and supplies, blockades and bridges and battle dispositions in the years when Napoleon overran Europe. There, too, are the still, sad realities of overpopulation, poor-laws, corn-laws, and emigration. And through all that mixture of the theoretical and the practical, the grand and the mean, the timeless and the timely, runs steady interest in the arts. Naturally, in a periodical owned by the publisher Murray and conducted by the critic Gifford, the attention paid to the structural and plastic arts is outweighed by the stress on literature. The articles edited by Gifford deal with literatures written originally in eight different languages. In short, *The Quarterly Review* touches, in a remarkable number of places, the early nineteenth century's great chains of being and of thought.

If the variety of subjects treated is wide, the variety of review writers is even more astonishing. For this period of fifteen years that included Corunna, Lake Erie, Waterloo, Peterloo, and the death of George III, 115 different reviewers are identified. But the distribution of articles among those 115 contributors is very unequal. That is, instead of each man's writing about half a dozen articles, nearly half (53) of the total number of contributors wrote only one article each. And 30-odd others wrote only two or three apiece. Thus slightly more than three-fourths of the men—there were no women—wrote less than one-fourth of the articles.

Yet those eighty-seven who contributed relatively little are not necessarily to be considered little men. Though some of them have been forgotten, many were figures in their day. The briefest catalogue of even a third of their names will illustrate the point. Grosvenor Bedford was Southey's intimate and trusted friend in London. William Erskine, Lord Kinneder, was close associate of Walter Scott in Edinburgh. And Frank Sayers, school-fellow of Nelson and of William Taylor the Germanist, was a poet, a philosopher, and an antiquarian of the distinguished group at Norwich. James Henry Monk and Peter Elmsley, clergymen, were both excellent classicists; the latter helped Sir Humphrey Davy in his work with the charred papyri of Herculaneum. The number of clerical contributors included John Brinkley, the first Royal Astronomer of Ireland, who later became Bishop of Cloyne. Perhaps just as interesting as the notables whom the Church of England saw fit to honor were the unrewarded Irish cleric, novelist, and dramatist Maturin and the proselyte Spanish-Englishman Blanco White. Both shared too little of Coleridge's artistic and critical talents, along with too much of his temperament. A Whig, too, as well as an apostate priest, could now and then be admitted to this company of Tory reviewers. For example, Gifford accepted and gladly published a philosophic paper by Macvey Napier, later editor of *The Encyclopaedia Britannica* and the successor to Jeffrey in 1829, as conductor of the Whiggish *Edinburgh*. Napier was of course only one of a reasonable sprinkling of Whigs. The young physician Robley Dunglisson's later career makes him, too, seem odd among the Anti-Jacobins. He was to emigrate to republican United States in 1825, and spend more than forty years as Professor of Medicine at the University of Virginia, the University of Maryland, and the Jefferson Medical College. In contrast with that young doctor, Stratford Canning, cousin of the great George, came to America about the same time. But he came as the British Government's Minister Plenipotentiary to Washington, and stayed only a few years. No doubt Stratford Canning's many and distinguished missions outside England minimized his opportunities to contribute to the Tory periodical that he had helped to found. Also in this procession of contributors of few articles are John Hoppner, court painter and portrayer of notables; Agar-Ellis, who sponsored the purchase and nationalization of some of England's great art collections; Whately of Oxford, who was soon to help shape Newman's mind at Oriel College; Henry Taylor, later of the Colonial Office, who was to write *Philip van Artevelde;* Sharon Turner, the Anglo-Saxon historian; and Henry John Stephen, a legal writer, uncle of the later Leslie Stephen of the *Dictionary of National Biography.* It was H. J. Stephen—not Croker nor Ward—who wrote the first article on Miss Edgeworth, about which some discussion has recently taken place. And it was the little-known poet E. S. Barrett— rather than James Russell—who produced the article on Hazlitt's *English Poets.* All those and more come flocking back to mind, though some of their names are rased, or missing quite, from the book of national biography. But the few more that we shall mention certainly need no muse to recall them: Henry Hallam, the medievalist, father of Tennyson's friend; Huskisson, the Tory statesman, who was to lose his life in a trial run on one of England's earliest railroads; John Hookham Frere, one-time Anti-Jacobin satirist, later the British Government's chief ambassador on the Peninsula at the time of Moore's death at Corunna, and still later the translator of Aristophanes' comedies; Malthus, the writer on population; Sir Thomas Stamford Raffles of Singapore, whose name has taken a new lease in recent years; and Charles Lamb, whose friendly article on Wordsworth seemed to his partial eye grossly mutilated by Gifford in the printing. Though the long night has perhaps been kinder to Elia's reputation than to the others, obviously the eighty-seven contributors of three articles or less were—not a few of them—men of mark in various fields of activity.

As already suggested, the other twenty-eight men produced the rest of the identified articles. That is, less than a fourth of the men are responsible for roughly three-fourths of the material. Within even that small fourth, the distribution is very unequal. Some seventeen of them wrote between four and ten articles apiece. Those seventeen writers include the classicists Blomfield and Mitchell, who carried on in the early nineteenth century some of the high reputation for scholarship that England had gained in the eighteenth century through such men as Bentley and Porson. The erratic wit, statesman, and critic John William Ward (Earl of Dudley, one of the richest men in England) ranged in subjects from Roscoe and Horne Tooke to Samuel Rogers and Miss Edgeworth. Robert Grant, who later became governor of Bombay, wrote brilliant articles on India, Crabbe, contemporary political conditions, and the characters of Fox and Pitt. His anonymity was carefully guarded, and his name was seldom written even in the confidential correspondence between the editor and the owner of the periodical. Captain George Procter, later colonel and historian, wrote chiefly on military affairs. The antiquarian and curiosity-seeker Isaac D'Israeli, father of the Victorian novelist and prime minister, wrote, among other things, an excellent survey of eighteenth-century periodical literature. Francis Cohen, later Palgrave, the historian and deputy keeper of public records, wrote on northern antiquities, folklore, and architecture. Chenevix, Irish chemist who made early experiments with palladium, wrote articles on France, especially on French literature, for both Whig and Tory quarterlies. John Taylor Coleridge, who for a brief time succeeded Gifford as editor of *The Quarterly* and later became a distinguished judge, wrote usually on contemporary English literary figures: on Milman, Mrs. Hemans, Barrett, Payne, Shiel, Shelley, and his own uncle, Samuel Taylor Coleridge. Copleston, Oxford Professor of Poetry and intimate friend of Ward, ranged from economics, ecclesiastical issues, and educational policy to a delightful critique on Whitaker's Latin history of the Rising of 1745. And last out of this class of seventeen, Nassau Senior, prophet of modern capitalism, published single essays on corn-laws and on literary copyright, and a series of three excellent articles on the then anonymous Scott novels:—five essays, in the space of one calendar year.

The next rather arbitrary grouping of writers, still smaller in number but more copious in production, furnished some of the most significant material that Gifford published. The seven writers in this group wrote between eleven and thirty articles apiece. Scott's nineteen place him about midway in this class. But two big gaps occur in the list of his contributions; the first is from 1811 to 1815, and the other from 1818 to 1824—a total of more than ten years in which he furnished nothing. And neither the length of his articles nor the quality is steady. Sometimes he dealt with his old love, balladry; at others, the poetry of Southey, Campbell, and Croker; and twice, after the death of George Ellis in 1815, the poetry of Byron. His four essays on novels include one (collaboratively written) on his own *Tales of My Landlord*. His other main subject, Scottish history, is well exemplified in the essay on the Culloden Papers. George Ellis, editor of early English poems and romances, wrote as a whole or in part twenty-six articles. This friend of Scott repeatedly during the last six years of his life reviewed Scott's poems and Byron's. His early connection with the West Indies and with Russia provided background for his essays upon those contrasted subjects. And his early and intimate and lasting connection with George Canning brought about a fortunate collaboration on such important topics as the conduct of the war in Spain, the Catholic issue, and the currency question, upon all of which the Tory periodical in its formative years felt the necessity of commenting. George Canning himself, another old Anti-Jacobin, was politically the great man of *The Quarterly*. Though temporarily inactive in the Tory government during most of Gifford's editorship of *The Quarterly*, Canning was shortly after to occupy the highest position in the party. Naturally his connection with the articles was the most jealously guarded of the periodical's secrets. Only one article, on national education, is assigned to him alone. And his exact share in the ten collaboratively produced articles—some of which have just been alluded to—can perhaps never be determined. Though politics was, from the beginning, an important element in *The Quarterly*, the sciences, as already suggested, also had a pronounced stress. Thomas Young, the main scientific contributor during Gifford's regime, had an amazing Baconian mind. His twenty-two articles show him a master of sciences, both theoretical and practical. He included chemistry, astronomy, physics, natural history, medicine, and the science of philology. He dealt with *The Herculanensia,* with Adelung on language, with Goethe on colors, with insanity, and with agricultural chemistry, the dew, and the tides. In this same quantitatively based classification, along with Scott, Ellis, Canning, and Young, come three admirable clerics. Reginald Heber the hymnologist, who became Bishop of Calcutta, sometimes took as his subjects travels in Egypt and the Near East and in Russia. The article on Madame de Staël's *Germany* is his. And among his eighteen articles are also accounts of Southey's history of Brazil; Byron's dramas and Mrs. Tighe's *Psyche;* and English translations of Pindar and Tasso. George D'Oyly's narrower specialty of sermons, theology, and translations of the Bible served *The Quarterly* well over a long period of years. His articles number fourteen. T. D. Whitaker's twenty-nine articles included also sermons and theology. But they ranged farther, in ecclesiastical architecture, Saxon antiquities, British local history, and natural history. And the excellence of his biographical studies, which are mainly on clerics, caused Gifford to pronounce him superior to Southey in character portrayal. His account of Jeremy Taylor and Melanchthon, with its fineness of insight and breadth of grasp, does contain many of the virtues of Southey at his best. Indeed, a good many of the essays produced by this small group of seven merit the praise that Gifford was quick to give to his best writers.

The most valued writers are still to be mentioned. This final group is very small, only four men. But they—Southey, Croker, Barrow, and Gifford the editor—constitute the inner circle of *Quarterly* reviewers. Together they wrote some 275 articles. Robert Southey, poet-laureate, during most of the period under discussion and writer of fifty-eight articles, commanded a wide range of subject-matter. Though he wrote upon English poetry, those papers were not his most numerous. His early residence in Portugal and his long-continued preoccupation with the history of Brazil made him an authority on the literature and the history of Spain, Portugal, and South America. Travels, too, interested this most domestic of men—travels by map or card, like those of Burton. Throughout the period under discussion he continued his articles on far places, notwithstanding Barrow's wider experience and greater scientific knowledge. Three other great interests were biography, the history of religious sects and movements, and social problems. His biographical articles on Nelson and Wesley were later expanded into the widely known books on those men. The first part of his almost epic account of Wellington, utilizing Southey's knowledge of the Peninsula, appeared within a week of Waterloo; and before the year was ended, the second part brought the narrative of Europe Delivered up through the triumph, utilizing in full detail Southey's first-hand observations at Quatre Bras. When Southey discussed Wellington among his cheering soldiers or Wesley among the singing colliers, his essay was not merely on a moment and a man. In it one feels a movement and a force —indeed, a motion and a spirit that impels. It is a part of a historical development, with its past, its present, and its probable future. His treatment of the rise and significance of British Methodism, though generous to individuals and in some degree even sympathetic, nevertheless shows the distrust of sect characteristic of this defender of the Anglican faith. On the other hand, when dealing with the foreign missions of the dissenters, where there was no great traditional Establishment to be endangered, the cause of missions was the cause of Christianity, as well as of humanity; and his interpretation was unembarrassed. Though the Pantisocrat and the writer on Wat Tyler had become the laureate of England, he had not forgotten his early social vision. Indeed, it had changed; but in doing so it had possibly become deeper and richer. Some of the most interesting subject-matters in his essays, for the reader of today, are found in the broad plain where the religious, the educational, and the economic issues meet and fuse into the great social problems brought to a head by the industrial revolution. Southey's *Quarterly* articles on England's social problems, begun in 1813, were continued in 1816 and 1817, and were doubled in 1818. At opposite poles, as they were, from the *laissez-faire* and utilitarian and statistical economists' approach, they in some measure anticipate the paternalistic socialism of Carlyle and Ruskin, and perhaps suggest even some of the twentieth century's efforts to deal with poverty and unemployment. With Southey's variety and mastery of subject-matters, his broad historical perspective on contemporary institutions and activities, his ability to give finely drawn and at the same time well-rounded portraits of the most different human characters, his uniformly serious consideration of the issues of life, and his pleasing and varied and effective literary style—with all those virtues, no wonder that the Poet-Laureate was one of *The Quarterly's* most valued contributors. No wonder that, imperfect as was the relation between him and Gifford, Gifford called him the sheet-anchor of *The Quarterly*. And no wonder that, in one out of every four numbers of the periodical, Gifford printed Southey's contribution in the leading position.

The contributions of John Wilson Croker, First Secretary of the Admiralty, appeared in seventy-nine articles. This poet, scholarly editor, political figure, and later subject of Disraeli's and Thackeray's satirical pens, was—except for his colleague Barrow—the most frequent and constant *Quarterly* reviewer under Gifford. His special province was recent French history. A magnificent collection of printed materials on the French Revolution, supplemented by visits and personal interviews on the grounds with eye-witnesses of events, enabled him to write with perfectly confident authority on what Carlyle was soon to pronounce the most notable practical phenomenon of the age. Books of memoirs, whether French or English requiring close familiarity with various parts of the eighteenth-century scene, were prime materials for this future editor of Boswell. In literature too, any British oldster who had not shown true asbestos in the furnace of 1793-1802, or any youngster who had not proved himself most loyally when put on in the years after Amiens, was likely on occasion to feel the sharpness of Croker's attack. Essayists or travellers or poets or fictioneers who like Godwin and Lady Morgan seemed to him to have carried French cargo or to have flown the buff-and-blue too brazenly; or who like Leigh Hunt and Edgeworth père and Byron's friend Hobhouse had admitted lack of reverence for the ark of the tabernacle; or who like Keats and Shelley and Mary Shelley had associated with known corruptors of aesthetic or personal or political character—any such writers might be subjected to search, ransacked for contraband, and hung up in *The Quarterly's* pillory as blasphemers against the bright lyrist Apollo, or Minerva or Vesta, if not against Britannia the Invincible. When such "fools" were to be cut up in slash reviews, Croker was the reviewer who could do it with effect and who would do it with relish. The technique of slash reviewing was of course not peculiar to him. But it was more characteristic of his short reviews—they were reviews, not essays—than of any other main *Quarterly* figure besides Gifford. Striking as those pieces may be, they were, however, only a fraction of his whole contribution; and we must include that consideration as we make our tally. Croker could and did intersperse his valuable historical studies and his scathing literary reviews with articles of sober insight into Edgeworth fille's *Tales* (second series, not first) ; into Scott's then anonymous novels; and into Lord Elgin's then unaccepted marbles from the Parthenon. And in his varied doings Croker unquestionably exercised important influence upon the course of *The Quarterly*. During the early years, the influence went indirectly, partly through his short articles, which made easily imitable models for unformed writers, and partly through his correspondence with Murray. Though Croker's relations with Murray the owner were close, his connection with Gifford the editor seems not to have been intimate. One is surprised; for Gifford surely depended upon him not only as writer of certain important sorts of articles but also as the periodical's only close tie, for many years, with the Government. During the last years of Gifford, Croker's direct influence became more palpable. In addition to his continuing as a regular contributor, he several times assumed, and discharged effectively, heavy editorial responsibilities while Gifford was temporarily incapacitated by illness.

John Barrow wrote wholly or in part the amazing total of 112 articles. About half of that number are now attributed to him for the first time, on the basis of manuscript authority. While Croker, the Admiralty's First Secretary, dealt mainly with history, memoirs, and literature, this Second Secretary, wrote on the almost boundless field of travel and exploration. Barrow's first trip as a boy to Greenland in a whaler, his long trips in manhood to China and South Africa, in responsible position with Macartney, and his residences in those last two countries had given him what was then, and would be now, rare knowledge of distant lands, peoples, and languages. For he had observed as a naturalist, as an anthropologist, and as a philologist. With wide reading to supplement his own travels and good sense, he could make what was ostensibly a review of Mungo Park's pathetic journal a survey of most that was known—or believed—in 1815 concerning the lower river system of the Dark Continent. During the period of Belzoni's excavations, Henry Salt's communications from Egypt enabled Barrow to write with special information on the explorations of the Pyramids. Another phase of his linguistic interest and ability is exemplified in his article introducing English readers to the Chinese language. That essay seems the more remarkable when we realize that, at the time, the only Chinese dictionary available in London was one in manuscript at the India House. At the opposite pole from his presentation of the laws governing Chinese orthography is his comment on the unexploited wealth of forest and soil and stream in America's hinterland. That is, a century and a quarter before the Tennessee Valley Authority, Barrow saw in his mind's eye the possibility of developing by inland waterways, one of the most important possessions of the globe, where then ran wilderness roads from the eastern mountains to the mid-continental river. (Perhaps it is worth saying here that the editor through whose hands such articles passed on their way to publication was not too much in sympathy with liberal views concerning recently rebellious subjects of His Majesty the King.) Barrow's informed and enthusiastic discussions of Arctic explorations are permanently commemorated in such place names as Point Barrow, Cape Barrow, and Barrow Strait. And such writings caught the popular interest, too, as well as that of the explorers. For example, an article on the Northwest Passage was believed to have added some thousands of names to Murray's subscribers' list. Barrow's regular occupation at the Admiralty Office furnished motivation for another series of articles on other naval matters, especially on the materials, the designs, and the techniques of shipbuilding. And the Admiralty's reports of wrecks, desertions, and salvage, combined with Barrow's Pepysian energy and curiosity, enabled him to be the first compiler of the story of Pitcairn Island and mutiny on *The Bounty*. Some of the less central interests represented in this genial traveller's articles are slave-trade, paupers, emigration, invention, and the bullion question. Naturally, perhaps, his full, frequent, and varied contributions did not always satisfy the editor's sense of literary style. Nevertheless Barrow's wide interest and comprehension, his dependable industry, and his equable disposition—even if his views and his literary style did not always chime in sweet accord with Gifford's aims for *The Quarterly*—made the Second Secretary far the most copious contributor during Gifford's years of editorship.

Finally in this sketch we arrive at the written contributions of William Gifford—old Anti-Jacobin satirist, translator of Juvenal, commentator on early seventeenth-century dramas, and editor of *The Quarterly Review* from its beginning until 1825. Of course we cannot here discuss in any detail Gifford the editor. That is a topic for treatment in the proposed history of *The Quarterly*. But we must here discuss—though briefly—Gifford the writer. Actually the number of whole articles now attributed to Gifford alone is eight. In those few—some of them slash reviews of now-forgotten fiction and poetry—the most serious interest is Roman satire. However, Gifford's main significance as a *Quarterly* writer is not to be found in his individually written articles. It lay rather in the writing and revising he did on other people's contributions, in order to harmonize them with a perhaps vaguely defined but strongly conceived policy and pattern for the periodical. Though the editorial policy was not entirely of his making Gifford's special care was to keep it constantly in mind, and in practice. He appears to have read critically all the articles that were submitted. Some of them, which do not concern us now, he rejected and returned to their writers. But many articles that were accepted for publication required, he felt, more or less revision in order to heighten their suitability. He sometimes called upon other *Quarterly* associates with specialists' knowledge to aid him in his editorial task. Throughout the process, he seems to have assumed, with a few misgivings in some individual cases, the prerogative of using all the resources at his command to fit the articles to what he conceived as the purposes of the periodical. Therefore his hand appeared, in one way or another and in varying degrees, in many articles. Though our index shows, in addition to his own eight articles, thirty-nine others in which he took some hand, the thirty-nine are only some striking cases; for the index would have been very misleading if it had attempted to record under Gifford's name, as part author, all of the articles that he is known to have revised for publication.

Closer attention to some of Gifford's revisions, or collaborations, will help clarify his procedures. Sometimes the proportions of an article needed change. For example, an inadequately illustrated article might be supplemented by additional extracts from the book under review (Entry 718); an additional part might be inserted in another article for the sake of completeness (Entry 269); or, on the other hand, an overlong article might be condensed (Entry 512), or divided (Entry 562). Sometimes the summarizing critical judgment in an article needed change. For example, the expression of a harsh judgment might be sharpened (Entry 468). Sometimes, however, a much more involved change in matter or in manner was needed. For example, a reviewer's expression of his individual point of view on a public issue might need to be brought in line with the general policy that *The Quarterly* was supporting at the time (Entry 168); or, if the contents were eminently satisfactory and only the style was somewhat out of keeping with the periodical's standard, parts might be rewritten for the sake of effectiveness (Entry 31). Or special circumstances might even call for the most sweeping changes of all. For example, once when refusal of a slovenly written article would have been impolitic, Gifford seems to have reorganized the materials (Entry 429); or, finally, a brief article that seems to have lain in limbo too long to be returned and that may have been needed as a stop-gap, had its contents realigned and its tone changed (Entry 307). Since there is no evidence to show that the circumstances involved in the last two examples were regular in their recurrence, we may suppose that the extent of editorial revision exemplified in them was rare. On the other hand, there is no doubt that the circumstances involved in the other seven illustrations were more frequent in occurrence.

We must end this account of Gifford and the other *Quarterly* reviewers with at least a hint on the general significance of his editorial practice. As already suggested, the articles Gifford saw fit to alter were well paid for. When they were printed in *The Quarterly,* they bore no signature to connect them with their individual authors. Gifford's repeated insistence that all contributors be anonymous, not only to the general public but also as far as possible to the rest of the circle of contributors, has significance in this connection; for, though never praised, he was often hated for labors not his own. The fact that Gifford had no uniform practice of sending proof-sheets to the authors bears also upon the point. And the additional fact that so important a person as Peter Elmsley was not permitted to reprint an article must also be considered. From those facts, a fairly clear principle seems to emerge. That is, the *Quarterly* articles were considered entirely the property of the periodical; and that periodical—the periodical alone, rather than any individual reviewer—was responsible for whatever appeared in its pages. From that point of view, Gifford's practice becomes ethical and honest. True, Southey complained about Gifford of *The Quarterly,* as Carlyle later rebelled against Jeffrey of *The Edinburgh.* But Southey—Carlyle as well—was an individualist and a very sensitive author. Southey believed himself something of a prophet; he conceived his works in solitude and brought them forth with pains. He had little respect for periodicals as a publishing medium, and suffered them only because of financial necessity. No wonder he became irritably articulate when he believed that his vision from the guarded mount had been clipped and fitted to the conventional policies of a party or to the standards of an editor of inferior insight. But while Southey complained of revision, Scott invited and welcomed it; Croker accepted it, perhaps without grace but also without resentment; and Barrow, so far as we know, raised no objection. That is enough on the point. Our purpose here is merely to indicate important facts of Gifford's practice of revision and to suggest an explanation of it, rather than to defend it. Without at least this meager understanding of it, one cannot realize the important but very complicated significance of Gifford's written contributions in *The Quarterly Review.*

That, then, is the rapid and general view of *The Quarterly's* contents and contributors during Gifford's editorship. The ins and outs of attributions of articles to individual writers will follow, after we have explained the rather simple mechanics designed to make the materials most useful, and after we have used the opportunity this Introduction gives to thank some of the people and institutions who have helped us most.

As already asserted, the whole body of various information given in the text has been evaluated, to the best of our ability, for ready use. That is, in the following pages we give first place in each entry to the author for whom the evidence seems strongest; and we record the evidence. Attributions that seem less valid are given next place, with their evidence, or sponsors. And so on. In order to save space, only manuscript sources are regularly quoted; and the printed sources are merely referred to, by volume and page. And both manuscript and printed source materials are referred to under abbreviated titles (see pp. 95-103 for Bibliography, arranged alphabetically under abbreviations). In the entries, authorities referred to singly, without explanatory quotations or digests, quite specifically attribute the article under consideration to the reviewer(s) whose unquestioned name(s) they follow. Authorities referred to in a group, after the italicized words *See also,* supply somewhat less definitive, but frequently highly important, evidence bearing on authorship of that article. For example, a reviewer's own printed letter saying that he had written a specific article and sent it on to Gifford for *The Quarterly* would have to be mentioned after *See also;* for a number of such prospective articles were eventually rejected by Gifford and his editorial associates.

Immediately after the Identification of Contributors occurs the full list of the fifty-seven unidentified articles.

An index to the present volume lists alphabetically all the reviewers whose names are mentioned in the text. And for each reviewer, whenever the facts are available, the index furnishes full name, birth and death dates, and the serial numbers of all the articles with which his name has been connected in our text. Notice, please, that the type used for these numerals in the index is not uniform. The regular-type numerals show that the identification is positive. The italic-type numerals show that the identification is tentative or doubtful. Of course, to determine accurately the extent of any reviewer's connection with any particular article, the user of this volume must go from the index reference to the evaluated evidence furnished only in the text, in the serial arrangement of articles 1-733.

Finally, we have some pleasant obligations to acknowledge. Various libraries have helped make this study possible: the British Museum Library, the J. P. Morgan Library, the Library of Congress, the Library of the University of North Carolina, the Library of the University of Tennessee, the Maryville College Library, the MacMurray College Library, the Illinois College Library, the Library of the University of Illinois, and the Library of the University of Iowa. The librarians in those institutions have put valuable resources at our disposal and have shown us the courtesies that make for friendship as well as scholarship. The Modern Language Association of America (acting through the Library of Congress) has made available microphotographic reproductions of two collections of Southey's letters. Generous leaves of absence in London, to gather materials, were arranged in 1945 and 1946 by the military and the civilian authorities at Biarritz American University in France. To four educational institutions at Maryville, Chapel Hill, Biarritz, and Jacksonville we have owed support during the years we have worked with *The Quarterly.* And MacMurray College, through the good offices of President Clarence P. McClelland, has generously defrayed the expense of publishing this volume.

Other debts permit still more personal statements. Professor Kenneth Curry of the University of Tennessee has searched through his copies of Southey manuscripts and has graciously given us references and quotations to use in this study. We are especially grateful to Sir John Murray, of 50 Albemarle Street, London, and to his associates. In the winter of 1945-46, they welcomed a stranger and allowed him day after day to transcribe office records (at Gifford's desk) and to photograph Gifford's correspondence. Fine spirits have always presided in The House of Murray! Still our acknowledgments are not complete; for this study, like those that have preceded it on other subjects, goes back to a great teacher. Professor John Manning Booker of the University of North Carolina continues the influence begun upon one of us over a quarter of a century ago. It has compounded as the years have passed. It is the rich gift of one who gladly teaches.*

HILL SHINE
HELEN CHADWICK SHINE

MacMurray College
Jacksonville, Illinois

---

* Professor Booker died on March 12, 1948, some months after this Introduction was written.

A NOTE ON ARRANGEMENT

(For more complete information on the subject, see the Introduction.)

The body of this work is arranged exactly in the order of the articles in *The Quarterly Review* itself. But in the left-hand margin the reader will find a series of numbers from 1 to 733 inclusive. They number the articles in this volume and are the numbers the reader will find in the Index of Authors. The italicized numbers indicate doubtful authorship. There are no page references in the index.

The brief citations after each numbered entry in the "Identification of Contributors" are abbreviations for titles of books which will be found in the Bibliography and which the reader will find necessary to consult for the published works. The manuscript citations are brief and their sources are also indicated in the Bibliography.

For analysis of evidence the reader may consult the Introduction.

CONTENTS

IDENTIFICATION OF CONTRIBUTORS

IDENTIFICATION OF CONTRIBUTORS

Volume I, Number 1 (February, 1809)

1. Article 1. Affaires d'Espagne

ELLIS, GEORGE, and CANNING, GEORGE. Smiles, I, 118. *See also*
Holloway in *RES* X, 62

ELLIS, GEORGE. Murray Reg. Murray MS, Gifford to Murray, postmarked
Nov. 29, 1808: "...Mr. Ellis has readily undertaken the Spanish article...." Warter II, 145. Robberds II, 277. Graham 9: "George Ellis was
responsible chiefly..." Holloway in *RES* X, 61 and note 2. *See also*
Smiles I, 116

2. Article 2. Cromek's Reliques of Robert Burns

SCOTT, WALTER. Murray Reg. Smiles I, 152. Lockhart III, 56; IX,
276. Scott. Cunningham 315-16. *Gentleman's* XXI, 137. Douglas I, 130.
Graham 41. *CBEL* II, 987. Paston 8 and note 2. *See also* Smiles I, 117,
118-19, 190; Grierson II, 136; Warter II, 145

3. Article 3. Orford's Anecdotes of Painters

HOPPNER, JOHN. Murray Reg. Hoppner xxiii. Warter II, 145. *See also*
Smiles I, 118

4. Article 4. Lady Morgan's Woman; or Ida of Athens

GIFFORD, WILLIAM. Murray Reg. Addit. Note: "See Ellis letter 3d
Mar 1809." Jennings I, 100. Grierson II, 166 note; II, 284 note. Clark
184, 193, 196. Brightfield 332. *See also* Douglas I, 164 and note; Hoppner
xxvii; Grierson III, 2

5. Article 5. Grammars of the Sanscrita Language

TURNER, SHARON. Murray Reg. Smiles I, 152. Warter II, 145

6. Article 6. Translations of the Georgics of Virgil

PILLANS, JAMES. Murray Reg. Addit. note: "...J P's letter Dec 29 1808
among Gifford's." Murray MS, Gifford to Murray, [Jany 1809]: "I enclose the article on Virgil . . . This article is not quite correct; what it
wants, however, may be done in the Proofs." Notation on letter: "Inclos-
ing Pillans' article on Virgil's Georgics—for the printer...." *See also*
Smiles I, 123; Clark 178-79

7. Article 7. Zouch's Life and Writings of Sir Philip Sidney

D'ISRAELI, ISAAC. Murray Reg. *Gentleman's* XXI, 137. Graham 41

8. Article 8. Cockburn on the Old Testament

? IRELAND, JOHN. Murray Reg.: "? Dr. Ireland" Addit. note: "See W G's letter Feb 6" Murray MS, Gifford to Murray, [Feb 6, 1809]: "I send you the Drs which I have carefully corrected; & La Place . . . corrected in all but the pointing . . . I trust Dr Young will be a powerful combatant for us." Notation on letter: "Sending articles by Drs Ireland & Young."

9. Article 9. Curran's Speeches

ERSKINE, WILLIAM. Murray Reg. *See also* Smiles I, 118-19; 148; Grierson II, 176

10. Article 10. Laplace's Supplement to the Mécanique Céleste

YOUNG, THOMAS. Murray Reg. Murray MS, Gifford to Murray, [Feb 6, 1809]: see Entry 8. Smiles I, 152. Brande XXVIII, 157. *Gentleman's* XXI, 137. Young 206. Pettigrew IV, 21. *See also* Smiles I, 123.

11. Article 11. Pinkerton on Medals

ROBERTS, BARRÉ CHARLES. Murray Reg. Addit. note: "Feb 9 W G writes J M 'I send you a very clever article by Mr Roberts....'" Murray MS, Gifford to Murray, [Feb 1809]: "...I send a very clever article by Mr Roberts. . . ." Notation on letter: "Article on Pinkerton." Bedford p. xxxix; 336-55. Smiles I, 151. Warter II, 145. *QR* XII, 519. *DNB*

12. Article 12. Public Characters of 1809-10

GIFFORD, WILLIAM. Murray Reg. Cites Murray's marked *QR*

13. Article 13. Southey's Translation of the Chronicle of the Cid

SCOTT, WALTER. Murray Reg. Robberds II, 266, 299. Lockhart III, 56; IX, 276. Scott. Warter II, 307. *Gentlemen's* XXI, 137. Douglas I, 130. Graham 41. Paston 8 and note 2. *See also* Grierson II, 136; Smiles I, 118-19; Southey 245, 251; Warter II, 145

14. Article 14. Accum on Mineralogy

KIDD, JOHN. Murray Reg.: "Dr Kidd (Oxford)"

15. Article 15. Barrett's Life of Swift

SCOTT, WALTER. Murray Reg. Grierson II, 161, note; VI, 200 and note. Douglas I, 130. Graham 41: Scott? Paston 8 and note 2. *See also* Smiles I, 142; Grierson II, 146, 200 note; Warter II, 145

16. Article 16. Carr's Caledonian Sketches

SCOTT, WALTER, and GIFFORD, WILLIAM. Murray Reg.: "Sir W Scott." Murray MS, Gifford to Murray, [Feb. 18, 1809]: "I send you the whole of Sr John with the exception of p. 13 & 14 between which what little I have to say must come in. . . . I will certainly finish Sir John— perhaps two pages or certainly two and half will suffice." Murray MS, Gifford to Murray, [Feb. 20, 1809]: "The knight's absurdities are . . . gross and frequent . . . I am tired. Perhaps the enclosed are quite sufficient . . . Our friend's last scrap I do not understand. He appears to have mistaken Sir John . . . I thought of writing more, but tis impossible . . . You know mine comes in after p. 12"
SCOTT, WALTER. Murray Reg. Lockhart III, 56-57; IX, 276. Scott. Grierson II, 101-2 note. Smiles I, 146 and note. Douglas I, 130. Paston 8 note 2. *See also* Grierson II, 157-58; Smiles I, 117, 144; Warter II, 145
SCOTT, WALTER, and GREY, SIR CHARLES EDWARD. *Gentleman's* XXI, 137

17. Article 17. Account of the Baptist Missionary Society

SOUTHEY, ROBERT. Murray Reg. British Museum MS, Southey to Danvers, Jany 4, 1809: "I have been writing a long article for a new Review . . . What I have been writing for it is a defense of the Baptist Missionaries . . ." Murray MS, Gifford to Murray, [Feb 26, 1809]: "In Southey's article there are two slight alterations which . . . you might make. *Sieks* is in one place misspelt *Seeks*, and Pers*i*c should be printed instead of Pers*ian*." Cf. *QR* I, 225. Warter II, 144. Smiles I, 152. Cottle 242-43. Southey 577, 254, 257. Robberds II, 275-76. Grierson II, 196, 236 and note. *Gentleman's* XXI, 137. Graham in *PQ* II, 97. Clark 179. Holloway in *RES* X, 62. Simmons 129. *See also* Warter II, 114, 148; Southey 245, 248; 255; Grierson II, 160; Smiles I, 116, 117, 146; Wilberforce II, 264

18. Article 18. Vaughan's Siege of Zaragoza

ELLIS, GEORGE. Murray Reg.

Volume I, Number 2 (May, 1809)
Published at the end of May: Smiles II, 157

19. Article 1. Campbell's Gertrude of Wyoming

SCOTT, WALTER. Murray Reg. Hammond: "Wal Sco"   Smiles I, 159. Scott. *Gentleman's* XXI, 137. Douglas I, 130. Graham 41. Clark 236. *See also* Smiles I, 330

20. Article 2. Poyer's History of Barbadoes

ELLIS, GEORGE. Murray Reg. Murray MS, Gifford to Murray, [Feb 6, 1809]: "Mr G E has not read the Barbado book. He does not admire the article, which must be sent very civilly back, saying it is already in hand." *See also* Smiles I, 120-21

21. Article 3. Portugueze Literature

SOUTHEY, ROBERT. Murray Reg. Hammond: "Sou" Murray MS, Gifford to Murray, [May 1809]: "Southey's is better written than anything which I have seen of his. He wishes to see the proof on account of the Portuguese names." Cottle 242-43. Southey 577. Warter III, 125. *See also* Southey 255; Warter II, 148

22. Article 4. Gass's Voyages and Travels

PILLANS, JAMES. Though Murray Reg. ascribes the article to "J Barrow & J Pillans," both Barrow 500-502 and Brightfield 206 indicate that Barrow's first contribution appeared in *QR* No. 4. Murray Reg's. Addit. note: "See Pillans letter Apr 24, 1809."
BARROW, JOHN, and PILLANS, JAMES. Murray Reg. Addit. note: "See Pillans letter Apr 24, 1809."

23. Article 5. Madame Cottin's Amelie Mansfield

GREENFIELD, WILLIAM (alias WILLIAM RICHARDSON, or RUTHERFORD). Murray Reg.: "Rutherford." Addit. note: "? Wm Richardson. See his letter Apr 17/09 with W G's." Scott, who introduced Greenfield with great secrecy to Murray, calls him *Greenshields, Rutherford,* and *Richardson.* See Grierson II, 178-79 note, 183, 184 and note, 184-85 and note, 189. *See also* Cook in *Nineteenth Century* CI, 605-13; Seymour 173; Snyder 205, 232 and note; Corson 367

24. Article 6. Improved Version of the New Testament

D'OYLY, GEORGE. Murray Reg. Murray MS, Gifford to Murray, [May

1809]: "I have put up D'Oyly's excellent Article which shall go to the
press with Southey's." D'Oyly I, 24. *See also* Smiles I, 157-59
IRELAND, JOHN. Hammond: "Dr Ire"

25. Article 7. Cumberland's John de Lancaster

SCOTT, WALTER. Murray Reg. Murray MS, Gifford to Murray, [May
1809]: "John of Lancaster is very good—I hope Mr. S. is *perfectly correct*
in charging C with fabricating his quotations. . . . In want of the MS . . .
I have made two or three slight corrections at random." Hammond: "W."
Grierson II, 176-77 and note. Scott. *Gentleman's* XXI, 137. Douglas I,
130. Graham 41. Paston *Memoirs* 113. *See also* Smiles I, 117 and 148;
Grierson II, 284-85 and note

26. Article 8. Richardson's Memoir on Fiorin Grass

KIDD, JOHN. Murray Reg.: "Dr. Kidd"

27. Article 9. Translation of Persius

GIFFORD, WILLIAM. Murray Reg. Clark 194: Gifford?

28. Article 10. Lettres et Pensées du Prince de Ligne

ELLIS, GEORGE. Murray Reg.

29. Article 11. Memoirs of Percival Stockdale

D'ISRAELI, ISAAC, and GIFFORD, WILLIAM. Murray Reg.: "I Disraeli." Murray MS, Gifford to Murray, [May 1809]: "I intend to rewrite
Mr. Israeli's pleasant history of P. Stockdale." Murray MS, Gifford to
Murray, [May 1809]: "I send you almost all of Stockdale . . . I will
write to Mr D'Israeli about it."

30. Article 12. Sydney Smith's Sermons

IRELAND, JOHN, and GIFFORD, WILLIAM. Murray Reg. Murray MS,
Gifford to Murray, [May? 1809]: " I send the Dr [Ireland] . . . I shall be
very happy if it can be printed by tomorrow night, or Friday noon. In
which case, I would take it to the Dr., & read it together." Murray MS,
Gifford to Murray, [May 1809]: "C [Croker or Canning?] may see a
revise of Sidney [Sydney Smith], as I shall be with him tomorrow." *See
also* Smiles I, 150; Grierson II, 183 and note
? ERSKINE, WILLIAM. Grierson II, 183 and note
CROKER, JOHN WILSON. *Gentleman's* XXI, 137

31. Article 13. Drake's On Periodical Papers

D'ISRAELI, ISAAC, and GIFFORD, WILLIAM. Murray Reg.: "I Disraeli." Murray MS, Gifford to Murray, [May? 1809]: "As it appears that
Dr Drake means to add a second (fifth) vol. Mr D'I may reserve for his
final criticism any observation which may be laid aside at present." Murray
MS, Gifford to Murray [misdated Aug 1809]: "In the last line of . . . the
subjoined proof, I suspect that I have mistaken Mr D I." Attached to letter: half proof-page 406 of article on Drake, showing considerable revision to improve style; and some sentences are omitted. Murray MS,
Gifford to Murray, [May 1809]: "By omitting Drake's first paragraph,
that article will be improved—I think it reads well." Murray MS, Gifford
to Murray, n.d.: "Drake I will endeavor to make something of it possible
tonight—in its present state it is *confusion worse confounded*. I have torn
off the last leaf." Murray MS, Gifford to Murray, [misdated August 1809]:
"I must have the revises of Sicily & Drake as the proofs were so much
scribbled. . . ." Graham 41: D'Israeli

32. Article 14. Leckie's State of Sicily

WALPOLE, ROBERT, and GIFFORD, WILLIAM. Murray Reg. Addit.
note: "See W G's letter No 28." Murray MS, Gifford to Murray,

[May 1809, numbered 28]: "Sicily now reads pleasantly enough, but I have had a deal of plague with it. Walpole must be more careful in future." Murray MS, Gifford to Murray, [May 1809]: "I send Sicily—but take the proof with me as I wish to show it to the Dr [Ireland] . . . little to correct . . ." Murray MS, Gifford to Murray, June 30, 1809: "I could not find Mr Walpole . . . so he is unpaid." *See also* Smiles I, 157-58

33. Article 15. Stephenson's Linen Manufactures in Ireland

KIDD, JOHN. Murray Reg.: "Dr Kidd." Addit. note: "Oxford. See W G's letter (No. 22) May 1809. Dr K was assisted by the Irish Chancellor." Murray MS, Gifford to Murray, [May 1809, numbered 22]: "I could have wished that the little article of Dr Kidd's on the Belfast Linen had followed S. Smith. . . . I suppose the Lord Chancellor, as he took some pains with the Belfast papers, will expect to see the article . . ." [Thomas Manners-Sutton, Lord Manners, was Chancellor of Ireland 1807-27.]

34. Article 16. Parliamentary Reform: Cartwright and Clarke

Author not identified. Murray MS, Gifford to Murray, [May 1809], in tentative list of contents for *QR* No. 2, designates one article "Croker." Possible anticipation of Croker's *Talevera,* reviewed by Scott: see Entry 63

35. Article 17. Austrian State Papers

TURNER, SHARON, and CANNING, GEORGE. Murray Reg. Murray MS, Gifford to Murray, May 15, 1809: "You reproach me with Turner's first article . . . As for the present, I have carefully looked it over, & given it to Mr C—who will return it on Monday. If it was retained before, it was . . . on account of the gloomy & uncertain state of the Austrian contest. . . ." Murray MS, Gifford to Murray, [May 22, 1809]: "Surely S.T. must be out of his senses—Part of his Article . . . is aimed at us." Notation on letter: ". . . with Turner's article on Austria corrected . . ." Smiles I, 157-58. Marriott 145. Clark 271 and note: Canning and? Turner. *See also* Southey 269

CANNING, GEORGE. *Gentleman's* XXI, 137. *See also* Grierson II, 210 and note

ELLIS, GEORGE, and CANNING, GEORGE. Warter II, 149

Volume II, Number 3 (August 1809)

Published late August or early September: see Grierson II, 236 note, and Warter II, 164

36. Article 1. Pamphlets on West India Affairs

ELLIS, GEORGE. Murray Reg. Murray MS, Gifford to Murray, [Aug? 1809]: "G. Ellis, I have revised with all my care & it may be worked off." That statement may refer to Entry 46, on Spanish Affairs. Smiles I, 160

37. Article 2. Transactions of the Missionary Societies in the South Sea Islands

SOUTHEY, ROBERT. Murray Reg. Murray MS, Gifford to Murray, [Aug 1809]: "The discussion on the missionaries . . . S writes so small a hand that my eyes are scarcely equal to it . . ." Murray MS, Gifford to Murray, [Aug? 1809]: "If you prefer S's America to the Miss. in this number, it may be used. . ." Warter II, 164. Cottle 242-43. Southey 577. *Gentleman's* XXI, 137. *See also* Southey 255; Warter II, 136, 148, 151, 153

38. Article 3, Kidd's Outlines of Mineralogy

THOMSON, THOMAS, and GIFFORD, WILLIAM. Murray Reg.: "Dr Thos Thomson." [An erasure preceded that entry.] Cites Cooke's Mem-

orandum Book. Addit. note: "From Mem book in office, but See W G
June 18, 1809." [Two of Gifford's letters, taken together, suggest that
John Josias Conybeare's review, which was submitted first, was replaced
by another, but that a small part of the earlier article was used.] Murray
MS, Gifford to Murray, June 18, 1809: " I do not see why Dr Conying-
hams [Conybeare's?] Review of Kidd may not be used." Murray MS,
Gifford to Murray, Aug 9, 1809: ". . . I send you the first part of Kidd.
It is very splenetick and very severe, indeed most too wantonly so; I
hope, however it is just some of the opprobrious language I shall soften. . . .
Pray let me have Dr Conybeare's Review, for there is one paragraph of it
which I should like to insert. . ." Murray MS, Gifford to Murray, n.d.:
"On looking over the proof I find a passage (p. 73) which as referring to
Dr T. himself, he may not like to lose. I have therefore sent it altered
as I wish it should be printed. The last part of it I omit. . . ." Smiles I,
161-62. Clark 178. *DNB* (under Kidd)

39. Article 4. Paley's Sermons and Memoirs

D'OYLY, GEORGE. Murray Reg. Murray MS, Gifford to Murray, [Aug
1809]: "I was forced to beg him [Ireland] to look at Paley in the Coach,
& he has not yet returned it. I think it D'Oyley's best." Smiles I, 161.
D'Oyly I, 24

WHITAKER, THOMAS DUNHAM. Nichols xxix and note. Nichols'
statement is not perfectly clear: he may be attributing the article to Whitaker; or he may be questioning the attribution.

40. Article 5. Lord Valentia's Travels

SOUTHEY, ROBERT. Murray Reg. Addit. note: "From G Ellis's letter
Nov 5/09." Warter II, 164. Cottle 242-43. Southey 577. *See also* Southey
254, 255; Warter II, 148, 151, 153; Grierson II, 236, note

41. Article 6. Whittington on Gothic Architecture

WHITAKER, THOMAS DUNHAM. Murray Reg. *See also* Smiles I, 161

42. Article 7. Tales of Fashionable Life by Miss Edgeworth

STEPHEN, HENRY JOHN, and GIFFORD, WILLIAM. Dudley 13-14
(Feb 11, 1814): "I was preparing to make a vigorous defence of Miss E
from the canting hypocritical accusations against her on the score of religion, when luckily I bethought myself of turning back to the two former
papers on Miss E in the *QR* [i.e. Entry 42 and Entry 198], in which I
found this charge preferred with great earnestness and solemnity . . .
just at the same time, to my great surprise, [I] accidentally learnt from
Murray . . . that those passages were of Gifford's own manufacture, and
inserted (pro salute animae) at his particular instance in an article furnished
by that 'serious young man' the younger Stephen." Murray MS, Henry
John Stephen to Murray, n.d.: "I returned the 'Tales of Fashinable Life'
last week, and am much obliged to you for the use of them. Before I put
my review of that work into your hands I could wish to see the Treatise
on Practical Education by the same Author. . . . The loan of it for an
hour or two will be sufficient for this purpose." Murray MS, Gifford to
Murray, July 21, 1809: "I think young Mr Stephen's criticism will do
very well. It is much better than you gave me reason to expect. In short,
I see nothing amiss in it, & a few trifling alterations will make it pass
muster famously." Murray MS, Gifford to Ireland, [Aug 19 or 22, 1809]:
"Stephen will do well enough, perhaps." Murray MS, Gifford to Murray,
[Aug 1809]: "To Mr Stevens or Stephens as you spell it (pray correct
my address) I have mentioned the M.S. on Russia, & offered it to him.
It is now too late to write a new letter, and I shall at all events make no
scruple of using it if convenient & proper." *See* Brewer MS, **Murray to
Croker,** in Entry 198

CROKER, JOHN WILSON. Murray Reg. *DNB.* Graham 41-53. Brightfield *338,* 453. *See also* Smiles I, 161-62; Butler in *MLR* XXIII, 277: not by Scott; Grierson II, 237 and 510: not by Scott
GIFFORD, WILLIAM. *Gentleman's* XXI, 137
DUDLEY, JOHN WILLIAM WARD, LORD. Edgeworth I, 173

43. Article 8. Haslam, Arnold, etc. on Insanity

YOUNG, THOMAS. Murray Reg. Brande XXVIII, 157. Smiles I, 161. *Gentleman's* XXI, 137. Young 228. Pettigrew IV, 21

44. Article 9. Pinckney's Travels through France

Author not identified. Murray Reg. attributes article to "J Pillans," and cites Cooke's Memorandum Book. Later Addit. note: "Mr. Pillans' art. appears to have been omitted & one by another hand substituted. See W G. Aug 31, 1809." Actually, several Gifford letters bear on the matter. (1) Murray MS, Gifford to Murray, [Aug 1809]: "What if this Review of Pinckney should be better than our own?" (2) Murray MS, Gifford to Murray, n.d.: "Pillans' Article would have given displeasure to all our friends . . ." (3) Murray MS, Gifford to Murray, [Aug 1809]: ". . . I have read Pinckneys Travels . . . there is no comparision between the present & that of Mr P." (4) Murray MS, Gifford to Murray, Aug 31, 1809: Pillans' article was omitted, says Gifford, because its radical defect was incurable. *See also* Smiles I, 162

45. Article 10. Middleton on the Doctrine of the Greek Article

SAYERS, FRANK. Murray Reg.: "? Dr. Sayers." Addit. note: "Either this art. or No. 5 appears to have been written by a Mr Stephens. See W G's July 21, 1809—See also W G's letter No. 35. See also No. 38x." [Article 5 has been otherwise accounted for. W G's letter of July 21, 1809, and his letter of Aug 1809 (numbered 35) have been quoted under Entry 42.] Murray MS, Gifford to Murray, [Aug? 1809, numbered 38x]: "Dr Sayers was incorrect in his quotations—and after looking through the whole of the Revelation (in Greek) for a *single* word which I could not find, I was obliged to send part of the MS to him." See *QR* II, 202 (No. 3, Article 10), for Greek quotation from *Revelation.* Robberds II, 294. *See also* Smiles I, 161-62

46. Article 11. Spanish Affairs: Sir John Moore's Campaign

ELLIS, GEORGE, and CANNING, GEORGE. Murray Reg. Addit. note: "In consequence of my importunity Mr Canning has exerted himself & produced '*The best article that ever yet appeared in any review.*' W.G. Aug 29, 1809." Murray MS, Gifford to Ireland, [Aug 19 or 22, 1809]: "I have heard from Mr G.E. He says that in consequence of my importunity Mr C has exerted himself & produced the *best article that ever yet appeared in any review.*" Notation on letter: "alluding to Quarterly article on Sr *Jno Moore.*" Smiles I, 160-61. Marriott 145. *QR,* CCX, 744-45. Grierson II, 236 note. Holloway in *RES* X, 62 note 3
ELLIS, GEORGE. Warter II, 164. *See also* Grierson II, 213, 249-50 note; Lockhart III, 63; Southey 255, 257, 259; Warter II, 149, 151

Volume II, Number 4 (November 1809)
Published December 1809: Smiles I, 168

47. Article 1. Rose's Observations on Fox's History

MEADOWBANK, ALEXANDER MACONOCHIE-WELWOOD, Lord. Murray Reg.: "Ld Meadowbank"

48. Article 2. De Guignes' Voyages à Peking

BARROW, JOHN. Murray Reg. Addit. note: "? J. Pillans whose letter (1809? April) see." Barrow 500-2. Smiles I, 166. Brightfield 206. *See also* Smiles I, 165 and 169; Clark 176

49. Article 3. Jerningham's Alexandrian School

IRELAND, JOHN. Murray Reg. Addit. note: "W G's letter June 18, 1809." Murray MS, Gifford to Murray, June 18, 1809: "Dr Ireland will take up Jerningham's School of Alexandria."

50. Article 4. Poems, by the Rev. W. L. Bowles

HOPPNER, JOHN, and GIFFORD, WILLIAM. Murray Reg. Graham 41. *See also* Clark 187-88; 273, note 98

51. Article 5. Ker Porter's Travels in Russia

HEBER, REGINALD. Murray Reg. Cites Murray's marked *QR*. Addit. note: "See Ellis' letter Feb 1810." Heber I, 343, note. *Gentleman's* XXI, 137. *See also* Smiles I, 165, 169; Bedford xl, and 117.

52. Article 6. Wyvill on Intolerance

Author not identified

53. Article 7. Bawdwen's Translation of the Domesday Record

WHITAKER, THOMAS DUNHAM. Murray Reg. Murray MS, Gifford to Murray, [Oct. or Nov. 1809]: "Whitaker I think may now stand." Nichols xxix.

54. Article 8. Emily, a Moral Tale, by Kett

D'OYLY, GEORGE. Murray Reg. Murray MS, Gifford to Murray, [? Oct 1809]: "I think I have improved Kett [?] and added a little to its severity...." Murray MS, Gifford to Murray, [Dec 1809]: "I send De Guignes [Entry 48].... Either D'Oyly or the Dr [Ireland, Entry 49] should come next, then Bowles [Entry 50], then Southey [Entry 55]...."

55. Article 9. History and Present State of America, by Abiel Holmes

SOUTHEY, ROBERT. Murray Reg. Murray MS, Gifford to Murray, [pencilled date Nov 1809 probably should be March 1809]: "Mr Southey has sent his Article on America." Murray MS, Gifford to Murray, [Aug? 1809]: "If you prefer S's America to the Miss [ionaries] in this number, it may be used . . ." British Museum MS, Southey to Danvers, Dec. 14, 1809: "You will I think like my reviewal of the American Annals in the 4th Quarterly." Robberds II, 339. Cottle 242-43. Southey 577. Cairns I, 33 note. Clark 183. *See also* Warter II, 148, 151, 184; Southey 255, 263; Smiles I, 118-19, 168, 169; Grierson II, 136

56. Article 10. La Place: Réfractions Extraordinaires

YOUNG, THOMAS. Murray Reg. Brande XXVIII, 157. *Gentleman's* XXI, 137. Whewell II, 369. Young 371. *DNB*. Pettigrew IV, 21

57. Article 11. Florian's William Tell

STEPHEN, HENRY JOHN. Murray Reg.: "Stevens." Cites Murray's marked *QR*. Murray MS, Gifford to Murray, Dec 20, 1809: "Pray have the goodness to complete the address of the letter to young Mr Stephen & send it to him. It encloses the draft." *See also* Smiles I, 165

58. Article 12. Oxford Editions of Herodotus

PARKER, JOSEPH. Murray Reg.: "Parker of Oxford." Cites Murray's marked *QR*

59. Article 13. Northmore's Washington, a Poem

GIFFORD, WILLIAM. Murray Reg. Cites Murray's marked *QR. See also* Clark 183

60. Article 14. Dr Parr's Characters of Fox

GRANT, ROBERT. Murray Reg. Smiles I, 169. Frere I, 177-78. *QR* CCX, 758. Clark 176. *See also* Bedford 117; Smiles I, 165, 176; Heber I, 345
DAVISON, JOHN. Warter II, 419
FRERE, JOHN HOOKHAM. *Gentleman's* XXI, 138

61. Article 15. Warburton's Letters

WHITAKER, THOMAS DUNHAM. Nichols xxix. *Gentleman's* XXI, 138
PILLANS, JAMES. Murray Reg.: "? J. Pillans." Addit. note: "See also W G's letter Feb 19, 1809. See also J. Pillans Ap 25, 1809." Murray MS, Gifford to Murray, [Feb 19, 1809]: "Mr Barry Roberts has been kind enough to induce a gentleman of his acquaintance to Review Warburton." *See also* Bedford 117; Grierson II, 210

62. Article 16. Mr. Canning's Letters to Earl Camden

ELLIS, GEORGE; CANNING, GEORGE; and GIFFORD, WILLIAM. Murray Reg.: "G Ellis & Canning." Murray MS, Gifford to Murray, [December 8, 1809]: "This lost article I also found. It has alterations, but no addition at the end... I have... written myself a passage of some length to be introduced in the middle of it, which I think will be of service to the question. Pray send me by the Bearer another set of slips of the *lost* Article, mine is so scratched & bedevilled by myself, and another person that it cannot be made out. I will insert the whole changes fairly in their proper places...." Notation on letter: "Mr G E's Rev of Letters to Camden as returned by Mr C."

63. Article 17. Croker's Battle of Talavera

SCOTT, WALTER. Murray Reg. Murray MS, Gifford to Murray, [Dec 8, 1809]: ". . . I recd . . . a little thing from our friend of the North . . . It is the Battle of Talavera . . . It is nearly seven pages of Scots hand and the quotations are not inserted . . ." Murray MS, Gifford to Murray, [Dec 8, 1809]: "I... send you S." Notation on letter: "...Scott's Review of Talavera." Scott. *Gentleman's* XXI, 137. Douglas I, 130. *DNB* on Croker. Graham 41. *See also* Smiles I, 169

64. Article 18. Hayley's Life of George Romney

HOPPNER, JOHN, and GIFFORD, WILLIAM. Murray Reg. Murray MS, Gifford to Murray, June 18, 1809: "Hoppner . . . is very anxious to undertake Romney . . ." Murray MS, Gifford to Murray, June 30, 1809: "He [Hoppner] takes Romney . . . with him, which he is very anxious to review. . ." Murray MS, Gifford to Murray, [November 1809]: "Hoppner I can certainly promise this evening tho' I have had a deuced deal of wrestle with it." Murray MS, Gifford to Murray, [1809]: "I am now hard at Hoppner which I have to have ready for you tomorrow morning—." Hoppner xxiii

65. Article 19. Jackson's Account of Marocco

HEBER, REGINALD. Murray Reg. Cites Murray's marked *QR.* Addit. note: "See G's letter Dec 8/09." Murray MS, Gifford to Murray, [Dec 8, 1809]: "On my return I found a light article on Jackson which Mr H had sent express . . . I suppose it will make between 6 and 7 pages." Notation on letter: "Mr R Heber's article on Jackson's . . ." *See also* Smiles I, 165, 169

66. Article 20. Short Remarks on the State of Parties

ELLIS, GEORGE, and CANNING, GEORGE. Murray Reg. Murray MS, Gifford to Murray, [Dec 1809]: "Mr C was with me on Sat. I dare say we shall have something interesting from G.E. It must be the last Article, I believe." Marriott 145

Volume III, Number 5 (February 1810)
Published end of March: Smiles I, 176

67. Article I. Herculanensia

YOUNG, THOMAS. Murray Reg. Murray MS, Gifford to Murray, Feb 13, 1810 [post-marked Feb 16]: "Dr Young has set up a page of curious Greek with Fry's types, which he wishes to have inserted in his Article. . ." Notation on letter: "No 5 Herculanensia." Brande XXVIII, 157. *Gentleman's* XXI, 138. Young 230-38. Pettigrew IV, 21

68. Article 2. Dentrecasteaux's Voyage à la Recherche de la Pérouse

BARROW, JOHN. Murray Reg. Barrow 501-2. Smiles I, 166. *See also* Warter III, 11-12; Barrow discredited cannibalism. Cf. *QR* III, No. 5, p 38

69. Article 3. Sir Brooke Boothby's Fables and Satires

? SAYERS, FRANK. Murray Reg. pencil entry: "? Dr Sayer (Norwich)." Graham 41: Sayers

70. Article 4. Sir Francis D'Ivernois' Effets du Blocus

ELLIS, GEORGE. Murray Reg. Murray MS, Gifford to Murray, [Feb? 1810]: "I have this instant heard from G E. . . . A short article on D' Ivernois (about 6 or 7 pages) will be sent in a day or two."

71. Article 5. Miss Holford's Wallace; or, The Fight of Falkirk

HEBER, REGINALD. Murray Reg. pencil entry: "? Scott or Heber." Murray MS, Gifford to Murray, February 2, 1810: "I have detained Wallace, because I expect Mr. Grey to send for it at the request of Mr Heber." Murray MS, Gifford to Murray, [? 1810]: "The conclusion of Wallace I had condemned before your letter came." Murray MS, Gifford to Murray, [February? 1810]: "H [not clear] is finished, but I . . . want to look it over narrowly—it will make 6 or 7 [actually 6½] pages—which are perhaps too many. The proofs, I sent to Mr Heber by his desire . . . I will take care of the last leaf of which perhaps your suspicions are right."

72. Article 6. J B Leroy de Flagis's Etat de Russie

ELLIS, GEORGE. Murray Reg. Cites Cooke's Mem. Book. Murray MS, Gifford to Murray, [?1810]: "Russia is most admirable, and I see nothing that can be altered."

73. Article 7. Peyrard's Oeuvres d'Archimède

YOUNG, THOMAS. Murray Reg.: "Dr Young." Murray MS, Gifford to Murray, March 13, 1810: "The 1st proof is not yet returned from Woolwich . . . The note, I believe, is in the second, which is also gone. I had softened it . . ." Notation on letter: "In answer to my solicitation to leave out a Note reflecting on Playfair in an Article on Archimedes..." Smiles I, 176. Clark 178

74. Article 8. Churton's Life of Dean Nowell

WHITAKER, THOMAS DUNHAM. Nichols xxix
? SCOTT, WALTER. Murray Reg.: "W Scott??" Addit. note: "See W G's letter No 76." Murray MS, Gifford to Murray, [March 1810, Numbered 76]: "Scott's Article reached me this morning—it is an Ironical imitation of Dr Johnson." However, Article 8 does not answer that description; see instead Entry 90.

75. Article 9. Lord Grenville and Dr Duigenan on Catholic Claims

CANNING, GEORGE, and ELLIS, GEORGE. Murray Reg. Addit. note: See W G's letter Feb 9, 1810 & Nov [Mar?] 16, 1810 & G Ellis's Feb 2, 1810." Murray MS, Gifford to Murray, Feb 9, 1810: "Pray make up a little parcel for Sunning Hill. [Sunning Hill, near Staines, was home of Ellis]. . . . Dr Duigenan's Catholick Question, Lord Grenville's Letter— for an article on that subect." Murray MS, Gifford to Murray, [Feb? 1810]: "I have this instant heard from G E. The article is finished . . . it will be overlooked by C & will make about 18 pages . . ." Murray MS, Gifford to Murray, [?1810]: "I have a few alterations to make in the Cathol-Quest but I wait for the arrival of the proof sent to Staines." Murray MS, Gifford to Murray, March 16, 1810: "I have this instant recd the enclosed from Mr. C." Notation on that letter to Murray: "No 5 Dr Duigenan Article 9." The enclosure mentioned by Gifford is as follows: "Gloucesterlodge/Friday March 16 1810/My Dear Gifford,/Is 'Duign & Gnv' printed off? or would there be time for a small interpolation? If there would—I should like to see it." Signature torn off. Notation on the enclosure: "A note of Mr Canning to Mr Gifford inclosed in this state to J M." Marriott 146

76. Article 10. Thornton's Present State of Turkey

HEBER, REGINALD. Murray Reg. Addit. note: "See G E's letter Ap 4, 1810." Heber I, 347 and note

77. Article 11. Mémoires de la Comtesse Lichtenau

? D'ISRAELI, ISAAC. Murray MS, Gifford to Murray, February 9, 1810: "Send . . . the slips of D'Israeli's which I have engaged Mr——— [marginal note says: 'G E'] to revise at Sunning Hill."

78. Article 12. Sir P. Francis and Ricardo on Bullion

? COPLESTON, EDWARD. Murray Reg.: "? G Ellis." Addit. note: "See G E's letter Mar 8, 1810 & Ap 4." Addit. note (in pencil): "Coplestone wrote an Art in this No. See G Ellis Feb 1810." Murray MS, Gifford to Murray, March 13, 1810: "Pray be careful to remember that the anonymous writer of Ricardo is a *different person* from the anonymous writer of Parr." *See also* Smiles I, 176-77 and note
? ELLIS, GEORGE. Smiles I, 176 and note: probably Ellis
?GREENFIELD, WILLIAM (alias RUTHERFORD, or RICHARDSON)
Cook in *Nineteenth Century* CI, 612-13

79. Article 13. French Embassy to Persia

Author not identified

80. Article 14. Burges's Euripides

? MONK, JAMES HENRY. Murray Reg.: "Prof Monk?" Cites Murray's marked *QR.* Addit. note: "Uncertain."

81. Article 15. Sydney Smith's Visitation Sermon

? IRELAND, JOHN, and GIFFORD, WILLIAM. Murray Reg.: "? Ld Dudley (Mr Ward.)" Addit. note says: "? Dr Ireland. See Ellis letter Apr 4, 1810." Murray MS, Gifford to Murray, postmarked March 31,

1810: "I have seen the Dr [Ireland] & he laughs at the idea. Let us keep our own secrets, & we shall do well." Notation on letter: "Article on Sydney Smith in No 5 after my application to Mr G—to know if it were quite proper. J.M." Smiles I, 184, Ellis to Murray, n.d.: "Gifford, though the best-tempered man alive, is terribly severe with his pen; but S.S. would suffer ten times more by being turned into ridicule . . . than from being slashed and cauterized in that manner."

? DUDLEY, JOHN WILLIAM WARD, LORD. Murray Reg.: "? Ld Dudley (Mr Ward)" Addit. note: "?Dr Ireland. See Ellis Letter Apr 4, 1810."

CROKER, JOHN WILSON. Smith vi. *Gentleman's* XXI, 138

82. Article 16. Barrow's Voyage à la Cochinchine

BARROW, JOHN. Murray Reg. Cites Murray's marked *QR*

83. Article 17. Herbert Marsh's Lectures

D'OYLY, GEORGE. D'Oyly I, 24
MONK, JAMES HENRY, or BLOMFIELD, CHARLES JAMES. Murray Reg.: "Monk or Blomfield." Cites Murray's marked *QR*

84. Article 18. Lives of Nelson

SOUTHEY, ROBERT. Murray Reg.: "Robt. Southey." British Museum MS, Southey to Danvers, Dec 14, 1809: "Yesterday I received a letter from Gifford requesting me to review the great life of Nelson, and offering me 20 guineas a sheet to do it . . . The Life of Nelson is by Stanier Clarke, whose . . . laying unhallowed hands upon such a subject, I am desired not to spare." Murray MS, Gifford to Murray, [March 10, 1810]: "I have begun on Nelson: and though I have many erasures to make, I confess I think what remains very good." Warter II, 413; III, 283. Cottle 242-43. Southey 291 and note, 577. *Gentleman's* XXI, 138. *QR* CCX, 746. Clark 176, 179. *See also* Warter II, 180, 184, 185, 194; Southey 267; Smiles I, 177

Volume III, Number 6 (May 1810)

Published between July 3 and July 17: Two Murray MS letters from Gifford to Murray

85. Article 1. Staunton's Ta Tsing Leu Lee; or, The Laws of China

BARROW, JOHN. Murray Reg. Cites Murray's marked *QR*. Addit note: "? Barrow. See W G's letter July 3/10 'Beloe has been worrying Mr B for an Art on Sir G Staunton.' See Barrow's letter Mar 20/10." Murray MS, Gifford to Murray, July 3, 1810: "Beloe has been worrying Mr B for an Article on Sir G Staunton." Murray MS, Gifford to Murray, post-marked July 17, 1810: "The Chinese Pantheon . . . to Mr Barrow and a list of what books you want from Paris." Barrow 501-2. Smiles I, 166

86. Article 2. Walsh's Disposition of the French Government

? ELLIS, GEORGE. Murray Reg.: "? Mr George Ellis." Addit. note: "See W G's letter of July 6 [16?], 1810 & G E's Feb 1810 & Ap 4/10." Murray MS, Gifford to Murray, dated July 16, postmarked July 17, 1810: "I have put up & left on my table for you No 2 for Mr G Ellis & No 12 for Mr Elton."

87. Article 3. Murphy's [Maturin's] Fatal Revenge; or The Family of Montorio

SCOTT, WALTER. Murray Reg. Brewer MS, Murray to [Croker], n.d.: "Walter Scott gave us one or two [general] ideas upon Romances in his review of 'Fatal Revenge.'" Pfeiffer in *PQ* XI, 103. Scott. Grierson III, 257 note; XII, 338-39 note. *Gentleman's* XXI, 138. Douglas I, 160. Graham 41. Idman 314 note 11. Scott-Maturin 1

88. Article 4. Dr Milner's History of Winchester

WHITAKER, THOMAS DUNHAM. Murray Reg. Nichols xxix

89. Article 5. Dr Jones's Account of the Eau Médicinale

YOUNG, THOMAS. Murray Reg. Brande XXVIII, 157. *Gentleman's* XXI, 138, Young 228. Pettigrew IV, 21

90. Article 6. Pursuits of Agriculture, a Satirical Poem

? SCOTT, WALTER. Murray MS, Gifford to Murray, March 17, 1810: "The packet from Scott is this instant arrived—but I do not see how we can insert it, as I think we are full. However we will talk it over—I have not yet opened it." Murray MS, Gifford to Murray, [March, 1810]: "Scott's Article reached me this morning—it is an Ironical imitation of Dr Johnson." Murray MS, Gifford to Murray, March 17, 1810: "Mr Heber, who called here this evening, thinks Scott's Article should if possible appear on account of his name. If you are of the same opinion, let me know, and I will prepare it."

91. Article 7. Ramayuna of Valmeeki

TURNER, SHARON. Murray Reg. Murray MS, Gifford to Murray, [March 1810]: "I *have* the Turner." Murray MS, Gifford to Murray, July 30, 1810: "Before I left town, I put up the money for Mr Turner, Mr Symmons & sent it by the penny post."

92. Article 8. Stanley's Aeschylus

? SYMMONS, JOHN. Murray Reg.: "? J Symmons" in pencil. Addit. note in pencil: "There was an art in this No by a Mr Symmons." Murray MS, Gifford to Murray, May 21, 1810: "If you have not sent Mr Symmons the Letter to Bloomfield, pray let the boy take it immediately. He has returned the M.S. But I wish him to see the letter." Murray MS, Gifford to Murray, July 30, 1810: "Before I left town, I put up the money for Mr. Turner, Mr Symmons & sent it by the penny-post."

93. Article 9. Bishop Horsley's Sermons

D'OYLY, GEORGE. Murray Reg. Cites Cooke's Mem. Book. Addit. note: "from R C's Memorandum book."
WHITAKER, THOMAS DUNHAM. Nichols xxix

94. Article 10. Shee's Elements of Art

? HOPPNER, JOHN and GIFFORD, WILLIAM. Murray MS, Gifford to Murray, June 18, 1809: "He [Hoppner] promises to write to Rogers for the poetry of Shee, but intends to reserve the notes for himself. [Hoppner died Jany 23, 1810.]" Murray MS, Gifford to Murray, July 3, 1810: "I have look[ed] over Shee once more & made it, I think, a good article."

95. Article 11. Berwick's Life of Apollonius

MIDDLETON, THOMAS FANSHAW. Murray Reg. Murray MS, Gifford to Murray, Feb 2, 1810: "Dr Middleton's direction / Tansor / near Pandle, Northamptonshire . . . / Pray let Philostratus's Life of Apollonius go *immediately*. I am sure it will be *ably* done." *See also* Grierson II, 386-87

96. Article 12. Worgan's Select Poems etc.

ELTON, CHARLES ABRAHAM. Murray Reg.: "? Charles A Elton" in pencil. Addit. note: "See J. M's Mem Book." Murray MS, Gifford to Murray, postmarked July 17, 1810: "I have put up & left on my table for you No 2 for Mr G Ellis & No 12 for Mr Elton."

97. Article 13. Residence at Tongataboo

SOUTHEY, ROBERT. Murray Reg. Cottle 242-43. Southey 577

98. Article 14. Grahame's British Georgics

SOUTHEY, ROBERT. Murray Reg. Murray MS, Gifford to Murray, Feb 13, 1810: "I do not see any probability of indulging ourselves with it [Cromek's article on Grahame.] After Scott had resigned it so readily to Southey & I had no suspicion of anyone besides undertaking it, I wrote to him [Southey] more than a month since, that the work was at his service; —He had sketched out the plan of his review, which I approved, and I dare say . . . that his critique is finished." Cottle 242-43. Southey 577. Graham 41
? SCOTT, WALTER. Grierson II, 397 and note

99. Article 15. Memoires d'Arcueil

YOUNG, THOMAS. Murray Reg. Murray MS, Gifford to Murray, Ryde, Aug 8, 1810: "I have also heard from Gregory [?] this morning, & he speaks in raptures of Dr Young's D'Arcueil." Brande XXVIII, 157. *Gentleman's* XXI, 138. Pettigrew IV, 21

100. Article 16. Evans's Old Ballads and Aikin on Song Writing

SCOTT, WALTER, Murray Reg. Scott. *Gentleman's* XXI, 138. Douglas I, 160. Graham 41. *See also* Grierson II, 397 and note

101. Article 17. Scott's Lady of the Lake

ELLIS, GEORGE. Murray Reg. Grierson II, 322 note, 346 and note. Lockhart III, 110. Smiles I, 126. *Gentleman's* XXI, 138. Graham 41. *QR* CCX, 747. *DNB*. Hildyard 109

Volume IV, Number 7 (August 1810)

Published after October 6, 1810: Murray MS, Gifford to Murray

102. Article 1. Portugueze Observer

SOUTHEY, ROBERT. Murray Reg. Cites Murray's marked *QR*. Murray MS, Gifford to Murray, postmarked Aug 18, 1810: "I see no objection to beginning with Southey . . ." Cottle 242-43. Southey 577

103. Article 2. Leslie's Elements of Geometry

? YOUNG, THOMAS. Murray Reg.: "Dr Young." Addit. note: "See W G's letter July 29, 1810." Murray MS, Gifford to Murray, May 21, 1810: "Leslie I will have ready . . ." Murray MS, Gifford to Murray, postmarked July 29, 1810: "I sent by this day's post, Leslie to Dr. Y. I hope he will not be fastidious and condemn it." Murray MS, Gifford to Murray, postmarked Aug 18, 1810: "Leslie I have recd: Dr Young can find no fault with it except that it is captious, & that the introduction is severe, and not called for.—Of the Scientific part which I was anxious about, he speaks not ill. . ." Possibly Young edited rather than wrote this article.

104. Article 3. Péron's Voyage aux Terres Australes

BARROW, JOHN. Murray Reg. Cites Murray's marked *QR*. Murray MS, Gifford to Murray, August 8, 1810: "I recd. Barrow . . . I have made him read more smoothly." Murray MS, Gifford to Murray, postmarked Aug 18, 1810: "I see no objection to beginning with Southey [Entry 102] . . . Leslie [Entry 103] & Barrow [Entry 104] may then follow. . ."

105. Article 4. Alicia T Palmer's Daughters of Isenberg

GIFFORD, WILLIAM. Murray Reg. Cites Murray's marked *QR*. Murray MS, Gifford to Murray, postmarked Ryde, July 30, 1810: ". . . I forgot to bring with me the Novel of Isenberg—& I cannot finish my little critique without it . . . if you could get the work . . . & send it to me, I will complete it directly." Murray MS, Gifford to Murray, postmarked Aug 18, 1810: "Isenberg is so intolerably stupid, that I fear, I have made nothing of it:—however it is gone, & may fill two or three pages." Smiles I, 180. Clark 184, 189-90. Graham 41. *See also* Clark 187, 273 note 98

106. Article 5. Bible Society: Dr. Wordsworth, Lord Teignmouth, Dealtry, Spry

? D'OYLY, GEORGE, or ? IRELAND, JOHN. Murray Reg.: "Dr D'Oyly." Cites Murray's marked *QR*. Addit. note: "? DR Ireland. See W G's letter July 17, 1810." Murray MS, Gifford to Murray, July 17, 1810: "Dr Ireland wants *Dealtrie*. If it was sent to my house, it was left behind, & you may contrive to borrow another copy." Murray MS, Gifford to Murray, postmarked Aug 18, 1810: "The Doctor has an article, which I have told him to send to Fleet St." Murray MS, Gifford to Murray, postmarked Aug 28, 1810: " I could not get to the Dr this morning, so that I shall not have the pleasure of seeing you till Thursday. . ." *See also* Heber I, 345

107. Article 6. Mirza Abu Taleb's Travels

HEBER, REGINALD. Murray Reg.: "Regd Heber." Cites Murray's marked *QR*. Murray MS, Murray to Gifford, Sept 25, 1810: "Respecting the Abu [?] article for instance—Mr Turner told me his book was written by friend of his a Mr Green—I . . . sent it with [word not legible] Travels as you told me to Mr Turner. He . . . reviewed it . . . I was disappointed when I saw it in print." Murray MS, Gifford to Murray, [Sept 1810]: ". . . with two or three better things in your hand, you [insert] the Abu [?] Art. which we had agreed should not be printed in this No." Some words in each letter are indistinct.

108. Article 7. Wordsworth's Ecclesiastical Biography

WHITAKER, THOMAS DUNHAM. Murray Reg. Cites Murray's marked *QR*. Cites Cooke's Mem. Book. Nichols xxix.

109. Article 8. Memoirs of the Life of Huet

Author not identified. A guess would be: Ireland, John. See Murray MS, letters from Gifford to Murray (August 18 to 28, 1810) already quoted under Entry 106

110. Article 9. Dr Clarke's Travels in Russia

ELLIS, GEORGE. Murray Reg. Cites Murray's marked *QR*. Murray MS, Gifford to Murray, postmarked July 17, 1810: "I have . . . left *Clarke* for Mr G Ellis." Murray MS, Gifford to Murray, postmarked July 29, 1810: "Before Mr E has done with Clarke, I have a little anecdote for him—a correction of an error into which the traveller has fallen." Murray MS, Gifford to Murray, [Sept 1810]: "Sending payment for Ellis." Smiles I, 184. Pfeiffer in *PQ* XI, 106. Grierson II, 381-82 and note. *See also* Heber I, 344
SOUTHEY, ROBERT. *Gentleman's* XXI, 138

111. Article 10. Diary of a Lover of Literature

PILLANS, JAMES. Murray Reg. Cites Murray's marked *QR*

112. Article 11. Select Poems, from Herrick, Carew, etc.

FIELD, BARRON, and GIFFORD, WILLIAM. Murray Reg. Cites Murray's marked *QR*. Murray MS, Gifford to Murray, [Sept 1810]: ". . . Field's article . . . is lively and amusing . . ." Murray MS, Gifford to Murray, [Sept? 1810]: sending payment for Field
FIELD, BARRON. Graham 41. *DNB*

113. Article 12. Replies to Calumnies against Oxford

DAVISON, JOHN. Murray Reg. Addit. note: "(?Home Drummond see W G's letter) See W G's letter No 94 Sept/10." Later Addit. note: "Mr Copleston wrote an Art in this No. See W G Aug 28. . . . See also J M's letter to W G & G Ellis Sept 1810." Murray MS, Gifford to Murray, postmarked Aug 18, 1810: "It [a parcel] contains a letter from Mr Home Drummond of Scotland saying that he has altered his review of the Oxford business and sent it up." Murray MS, Gifford to Murray, postmarked Aug 28, 1810: "I have recd . . . a considerable part of the Review of Mr Coplestone, with a promise of the remr. [remainder] in the course of ten days." Murray MS, Gifford to Murray, [Sept 1810, numbered 94]: Gifford does not wish to affront Mr Davison by omitting his article now. Smiles I, 181-83. *Gentleman's* XXI, 138. *DNB*. Clark 175

114. Article 13. John Gifford's Life of Pitt

GRANT, ROBERT. Murray Reg. Addit. note: "Grant appears to have been a friend of Heber. Aug 17, 1810" Murray MS, Gifford to Murray, postmarked August 18, 1810: "—not a line from our unknown friend— I must apply to Heber." Murray MS, Gifford to Murray, ["Recd Oct 6, 1810"]: "Pitt is not yet come to hand . . . Mr C . . . is delighted with Pitt, indeed." Frere I, 177-78. *Gentleman's* XXVIII, 34. *See also* Heber I, 345

CANNING, GEORGE. British Museum MS, Southey to Peachey, Nov 27, 1810: "There are some bold strokes against the Scotchmen in the last number,—in the article upon Leslie & in that upon Mr Pitt, the main part of which comes (I have no doubt) from Canning." Romilly II, 359 and note.

DAVISON, JOHN. Warter II, 419: Southey believes Davison the author

FRERE, JOHN HOOKHAM. *Gentleman's* XXI, 138

Volume IV, Number 8 (November 1810)

Published late December 1810: *see* Grierson II, 428 note, and Murray MS, Gifford to Murray, postmarked Dec 20

115. Article 1. Crabbe's Borough

GRANT, ROBERT. Though Murray Reg. attributes article to "Wm Gifford?" Addit. note says "Robt Grant," and cites Murray's marked *QR*. "See also W G's Aug 6-7, 1810." Murray MS, Gifford to Murray, postmarked Aug 7, 1810: "Of Crabbe, he [Heber, the intermediary between the anonymous Robert Grant and Gifford] says, that he hears it is proceeding —but he has not seen any part of it." Murray MS, Gifford to Murray, [Sept 1810]: "Pitt, I am informed I shall have tomorrow. One sheet of Crabbe is come . . . I am promised two sheets more directly . . ." *See also* Grierson II, 397 and note

GIFFORD, WILLIAM. Murray Reg.: "Wm Gifford?" For Addit. note, see above, under *Robert Grant*. Murray MS, Gifford to Murray, [November 1810]: "Barrow & Crabbe I had been prevented from finishing by a succession of people calling . . ." *Gentleman's* XXI, 138. Graham 41. Huchon 305. *See also* Clark 187 and 273 note, 188, 191-92, and 200: Clark doubts Gifford's authorship.

116. Article 2. Patten's Natural Defense of an Insular Empire

BARROW, JOHN. Murray Reg. Cites Murray's marked *QR*

117. Article 3. Landt's Description of the Feroe Islands

SOUTHEY, ROBERT. Murray Reg. Cites Murray's marked *QR*. Smiles I, 182. Cottle 242-43. Southey 577

118. Article 4. Chalmers' Caledonia

WHITAKER, THOMAS DUNHAM. Murray Reg. Cites Murray's marked *QR*. Nichols xxix and xxxiv note 2

119. Article 5. Weston's Conquest of the Miao-tsé

BARROW, JOHN. Murray Reg. Cites Murray's marked *QR*

120. Article 6. Price on the Picturesque
Author not identified

121. Article 7. Musae Cantabrigienses

? FALCONER, THOMAS. Murray Reg.: "? Falconer." Addit. note: "Arts in this no. by Sayers and Falconer. See W G's letter No 103 . . . see W G 108+." Murray MS, Gifford to Murray, [Nov 1810, numbered 103]: "Falconer you may have in a day or two . . ." Murray MS, Gifford to Murray, [1810, numbered 108+]: "Mr H has seen Falconer & he thinks, as every scholar must, very highly of it." Murray MS, Gifford to Murray, [Oct-Nov 1810]: "I sent the Cam[bridge] verses yesterday. . ."

122. Article 8. Woodhouse's Trigonometry
Author not identified

123. Article 9. Sir Ralph Sadleir's State Papers

LODGE, EDMUND. Murray Reg. *Gentleman's* XXI, 138. *DNB*

124. Article 10. Huskisson on the Depreciation of Currency

ELLIS, GEORGE. Murray Reg. Addit. note: "see G E's letter Oct 3, 1810." Murray MS, Gifford to Murray, [Oct-Nov 1810]: "I have recd the pamphlets . . . in time for Mr C who has this moment taken then to Sunning Hill . . . I have also desired G E to hasten his first article. . ." Grierson II, 428 note

125. Article 11. Southey's History of Brazil

HEBER, REGINALD. Murray Reg. Cites Murray's marked *QR*. Murray MS, Gifford to Murray, postmarked Dec 20, 1810: "Mr H. has not yet returned the Brazils—which he wished to see & took last night. As soon as I get it back, it shall be corrected & sent!" Graham 41. *See also* Robberds II, 340; Warter II, 209, 307-8

126. Article 12. Britton's Architectural Antiquities

? SAYERS, FRANK. Though Murray Reg. does not assign this article, Addit. note says: "Arts in this No by Sayers & Falconer. See W G's letter No 103 . . ." Murray MS, Gifford to Murray, July 30, 1810: "I will look over Sayers . . . & send . . . by tomorrow's coach . . . Sayers, though well written, is not of much importance, I see; but he seems fond of it, and it can do us no harm." Murray MS, Gifford to Murray, Aug 3, 1810: "I return . . . Sayers." Murray MS, Gifford to Murray, [Nov 1810, numbered 103]: "I send you Sayers. . ." *See also* Robberds II, 294, 297-98, which supply important hints.

127. Article 13. Evangelical Sects: Hints to the Public and the Legislature . . . By a Barrister

SOUTHEY, ROBERT. Murray Reg. British Museum MS, Southey to Danvers, Oct 8, 1810: "I am reviewing the Barristers Hints. Of all the rascally writers whom I have ever [perused?] this is surely the most thoroughly dishonest & the most thoroughly impudent. I hope I shall make even his own party ashamed of him." Murray MS, Gifford to Murray, [December 19, 1810]: "I have recd . . . Southey which requires a few omissions only . . . I shall make all my emendations that is—erasures this evening . . ." Murray MS, Gifford to Murray, [December 1810]: "The Dr & I perfectly agree in the propriety of Southey's omissions & in those that we have made since—The Article is now safe as it is interesting. It has lost no part of its force." British Museum MS, Southey to Peachey, Dec 26, 1811: "Last night I received a singular & gratifying proof that in some of my late endeavours I have not altogether been labouring in vain. A circular letter was sent me from the Bristol Church of England Tract Society . . . The society is founded for the purpose which I recommended in the Quarterly Review, when treating of the Methodists, . . .— that of making the people acquainted with this history of their own church [see *QR* IV, 512-14] . . ." Warter II, 221 and 308: Southey says the article has been mutilated. Cottle 242-43. Southey 577. *Gentleman's* XXI, 138. *See also* Grierson II, 202 and note; Southey 259; Forster 214; Warter II, 149, 153, 191, 207, 249 [On p. 249 read *sects* instead of *poets.*]

128. Article 14. Miss Mitford's Poems

MITFORD, JOHN, and GIFFORD, WILLIAM. Though Murray Reg. says "Rev J Mitford," Addit. note says: "aided by W Gifford," and cites Murray's marked *QR*. Murray MS, Gifford to Murray, [Nov 1810]: "I send you . . . Mitford . . . which I have endeavoured to make something of." Murray MS, Gifford to Murray, [Dec 1810]: "Mr Heber is decidedly for Mitford, which he thinks a severe but sprightly article." *D N B*: by Mitford, much mutilated by Gifford. *See also* Hill 119

MITFORD, JOHN. Murray Reg.: "Rev J Mitford." Addit. note: "aided by W Gifford." Cites marked *QR*. *Gentleman's* XXI, 138. Mitford I, 54 note. Graham 41

SCOTT, WALTER. *QR* LVII, 323. Cf. *QR* IV, 516-17

129. Article 15. Observations on Bullion Committee: Sir John Sinclair

ELLIS, GEORGE; CANNING, GEORGE; and HUSKISSON, WILLIAM. Though Murray Reg. says "Geo. Ellis & Geo Canning," Addit. note says: "Nominally by G.E. Really by Canning & W Huskisson," and cites Murray's marked *QR*. Murray MS, Gifford to Murray, [Oct-Nov 1810]: "I have recd the pamphlets, & made them up in time for Mr C who has . . . taken them to Sunning Hill where he stays tomorrow & Monday." Murray MS, Gifford to Murray, [erroneously dated "? Aug 1811"]: "I have heard from C & from Sunning Hill & they have sent . . . suggestions for the last Article which they wish me to interweave . . . Sir J you shall have as soon as I have made the alterations which I only recd this morning." Murray MS, Gifford to Murray, [Nov? 1810]: "I have just recd notes from Mr E & Mr C respecting one *erasure* in the proofs of Sir John. . . The quotation is that from *Lear,* & is, I think, a speech of the *Fool. . .*" Murray MS, Gifford to Murray, [Dec. 19, 1810]: ". . . Mr C will call here to see that his marginal marks have been understood . . ." Notation on letter: "Q Rev No 8 article on Sir John Sinclair—returned with very considerable alterations corrections & additions by Mr C in his own handwriting—J.M." Marriott 146. Horner II, 68. *See also* Grierson II, 428-29 and note

ELLIS, GEORGE, and CANNING, GEORGE. Murray Reg.: "Geo Ellis & Geo. Canning." Addit. note: "Nominally by G.E. Really by Canning & W. Huskisson." Cites Murrays marked *QR*. *Gentleman's* XXI, 138. *QR* CCX, 744. *See also D N B* III, 875

? Partly by SCOTT, WALTER. Murray Reg's Addit. note: "W Scott had an Art in this No. See W G's letter 106." Murray MS, Gifford to Murray, [Dec 1810, numbered 106]: "The rest of Scott is come." Grierson II, 428 and note. *See also* Grierson III, 41 and note

Volume V, Number 9 (February 1811)

Published in March: Murray Reg.

130. Article 1. Clavier's Histoire des Premiers Temps de la Grèce

Author not identified. Murray MS, Gifford to Murray, [Feb 1811]: "I send you Clavier which I hope the printer will be careful of, as it is a presentation copy."

131. Article 2. Southey's Curse of Kehama

SCOTT, WALTER, and BEDFORD, GROSVENOR. Murray Reg.: "Sir W. Scott." Addit. note: "In Drawing Room vols [i.e. Murray's marked *QR*] this art is attributed to G. Bedford." Murray MS, Gifford to Murray, [Jan-Feb 1811]: "I have heard from Scott . . . He has sent Kehama . . ." Morgan MS, Southey to E. Elliott Jr., Feb 7, 1811: "Scott tells me he has reviewed it [my poem] for the next Quarterly." Warter II, 307 [Southey's letter to Capt. Southey, misdated Dec 5, 1812]: "Bedford has seen the review which Scott has written of it [Kehama], and which, from his account, though a very friendly one, is . . . very superficial. He sees nothing but the naked story; the moral feeling which pervades it has escaped him. I do not know whether Bedford will be able to get a paragraph interpolated touching upon this, and showing that there is some difference between a work of high imagination and a story of mere amusement." Murray MS, Gifford to Murray, [February 1811]: "[I am sending] some more of Scott—but I must make a few additions to its last pages, which I am now doing." [See *QR* V, No. 9, pp. 55 and 56, for three paragraphs on the relation of high poetic imagination and moral virtue: possibly Bedford's interpolation.] Smiles I, 189: Scott. Robinson I, 39: Scott. Heber I, 35: Scott. Grierson II, 409 note: Scott. Lockhart III, 110 and IX, 276: Scott. Scott: Scott. *Gentleman's* XXI, 138: Scott. Douglas I, 206: Scott. Graham 41: Scott. *See also* Smiles I, 190: Grierson II, 346, 409, 410, 415-16; Lockhart III, 110; Southey 272; Warter II, 210; Robberds II, 339; Forster 155

132. Article 3. Sir Robert Wilson's Campaigns in Poland

? HEBER, REGINALD. Murray Reg.: "? Heber" in pencil. Murray MS, Gifford to Murray, [? 1810-11]: "I have got a person for Sir R Wilson—a good one"

133. Article 4. Dr Whitaker's De Motu per Britanniam Civico

COPLESTON, EDWARD. Murray Reg.'s Addit. note in pencil: "Coplestone wrote an art in this No. See W G's letter no. 119." Murray MS, Gifford to Murray, [misdated May? 1811; numbered 119]: "Coplestone came today and will be ready at any time—Part of Aeschylus is come from Cambridge also today . . . P.S. Do not mention Copleston's name." Murray MS, Gifford to Murray, [1811]: "Dr I [sent?] last night for the last leaf of Dealtry and De Motu with a promise to send back both this morning. They are not come." Nichols xxiii and note. Copleston 347. *DNB. See also* Copleston 40

134. Article 5. Roscoe's Observations on Lord Grey's Address

DUDLEY, JOHN WILLIAM WARD, LORD. Murray Reg. Cites Murray's marked *QR*

135. Article 6. Hoare's Ancient Wiltshire

WHITAKER, THOMAS DUNHAM. Murray Reg. Cites Murray's marked *QR*. Murray MS, Gifford to Murray [March 18, 1811]: "I have not Mr Whitakers letter—if it does not come by tomorrow's post, it [the article?] must go as it is." Nichols xxix.

136. Article 7. Sir John Sinclair's Remarks

ELLIS, GEORGE, and CANNING, GEORGE. Murray Reg. Murray MS, Gifford to Murray, [March 18, 1811]: "Mr C will be with me on Wednesday . . . when Sir J will be finally discussed." Murray MS, Gifford to Murray, [March 25, 1811]: "Mr C wishes . . . to make a few trifling changes in Sir John . . . p. 130 135 136 137 138 . . ." Lockhart II, 379-81 and note. Marriott 146. *Gentleman's* XXI, 138. *See also DNB* III, 875

137. Article 8. India—Disturbances at Madras

GRANT, ROBERT. Murray Reg. Cites Murray's marked *QR*. Murray MS, Gifford to Murray, [Oct-Nov 1810]: "I have recd a letter from *Romney* to say that the *whole* of India will be with me on Wednesday, & part of it before—keep this secret, I mean the post mark." *See also* Warter II, 290

138. Article 9. Blomfield's Prometheus Vinctus

MONK, JAMES HENRY. Murray Reg. Murray MS, Gifford to Murray, [misdated "? 1811 May"]: "Part of Aeschylus is come from Cambridge also today—very good . . ."

139. Article 10. Grant's History of Mauritius

ELMSLEY, PETER. Murray Reg. Cites Murray's marked *QR*

140. Article 11. Tracts on the Bullion Committee

BARROW, JOHN, and CANNING, GEORGE. Murray Reg. "J. Barrow." Cites Murray's marked *QR*. Addit. note: "? revised by G. Canning See W G's letter No 111." Murray MS, Gifford to Murray, [undated. Probably early 1811]: "I sent the remdr of Barrows slight art." Murray MS, Gifford to Murray, [Feb 1811, numbered 111]: "I heard today . . . about the Bullion—I have all the sheets *this inst*[*ant*] returned from Mr. C. . . . I am glad the Bullion [Baltic?] follows Blomfield."
ELLIS, GEORGE, and CANNING, GEORGE. *QR* CCX, 744: "written in conjunction with his [Canning's] friend Ellis, and inspired by others. . ."

Volume V, Number 10 (May 1811)
Published in June: Murray Reg.

141. Article 1. French Translation of Strabo

FALCONER, THOMAS. Murray Reg.: "Rev Thos Falkner." Murray MS, Gifford to Murray, postmarked July 17, 1810: "The French Strabo must be sent . . . to the Revd Mr T Falkner, Bath." *Gentleman's* XXI, 138: "Falkener." *DNB*: "Falconer"

142. Article 2. Kirkpatrick's Account of the Kingdom of Nepaul

BARRY, HENRY. Murray Reg.: "? Mr Barry." Addit. note: "See W G's letter No 120 & 123" Murray MS, Gifford to Murray, [May 1811, numbered 120]: "I send you the first 16 pages of Barry . . . The rest tomorrow . . . the Revise is gone to the Admiralty as C [Croker?] wished to look at it." Murray MS, Gifford to Murray, [May 1811, numbered 123]: "I send the first page of Nepaul . . . the remainder . . . will make about 12 pages . . . Pray let this part of Nepaul be set up without delay." Murray MS, Gifford to Murray, [May 28, 1811]: "I think Barry [Baring?] will amuse. Can it be got in?"

143. Article 3. Lysons' Magna Britannia

WHITAKER, THOMAS DUNHAM. Murray Reg.: "? Dr Whitaker" in pencil. Nichols viii, xiv, xxix, xxxiv

144. Article 4. Dealtry's Principles of Fluxions

? D'OYLY, GEORGE, or ? IRELAND, JOHN. Murray Reg. "Dr Ireland D'Oyly" Addit. note: "See W G's letter No. 119 & 121." Murray MS, Gifford to Murray, [misdated May? 1811; numbered 119]: "I sent all of Dealtry but the last leaf which I am obliged to keep, because I have not yet seen Dr Ireland. This little addition must come in there." Murray MS, Gifford to Murray, [1811]: "Dr I [sent?] last night for the last leaf of Dealtry & De Motu . . . I told you that Dr I would positively reach me on Wednesday." Murray MS, Gifford to Murray, [May? 1811; numbered 121]: "D'Oyly has Dealtry and his own proof. . ." Murray MS, Gifford to Murray, [May 1811]: ". . . D'Oyly has not yet sent his proof." Murray MS, Gifford to Murray, [May 17, 1811]: "D'Oyly has not been sent but I think the first sheet will want few alterations . . ."

145. Article 5. State of the Established Church

? DRUMMOND, HENRY HOME. Murray Reg.: "?Drummond" in pencil. Addit. note: "See W G's Letter No 120. . ." Murray MS, Gifford to Murray, [May 1811, numbered 120]: "And we must see if we cannot foist in Drummond [into no. 10]"

146. Article 6. General Tarleton's Speech

CROKER, JOHN WILSON, and "MR B'S FRIEND." Murray Reg.: "J W Croker." Addit. note: "Croker revised this, but W. G. writes May 9, 1811 'it is not from Mr C. but comes from Mr B's friend." Murray MS, Gifford to Murray, [May 9, 1811]: ". . . review of Tarleton . . . is not from Mr C but comes from Mr B's friend." Murray MS, Gifford to Murray, [May 1811]: ". . . Tarleton . . . I like Mr Croker's alterations as far as they go, very much indeed." Murray MS, Gifford to Murray, [May 1811]: "Not knowing that Mr Croker was out of town I left both sheets at the Admiralty as Tarleton was divided between them." Brewer MS, Murray to [Croker], June 3, [1811]: ". . . Barrow . . . told me that he had sent the Sheet with Tarleton upon it. . ." Brightfield 453: Croker revised it only. D N B: Croker's second QR article was in No. 10

147. Article 7. Marshman's Dissertation on the Chinese Language

STAUNTON, SIR GEORGE THOMAS. Murray Reg. Cites Murray's marked QR. See also Grierson II, 441 and note

148. Article 8. Capt. Pasley on the Military Policy of Great Britain

SOUTHEY, ROBERT, and CROKER, JOHN WILSON. Murray Reg.: "R Southey." Cites Cooke's Mem Book. Addit. note: "Aided by Croker." Cites Murray's marked QR. Murray MS, Gifford to Murray, [1811]: ". . . Paisley . . . must go thru more hands than Southey's . . ." Murray MS, Gifford to Murray, [March 18, 1811]: ". . . Southey . . . is perfectly incorrect and dangerous . . . Southey's article [on Pasley] . . . would involve us in quarrels with all parties and commit the Review to principles which cannot be maintained . . . I must show it to some person or other . . . I must [consult] . . . one or other of our great men . . ." Murray MS, Gifford to Murray, [May 1811]: "I have looked over Paisley & like it very much; but I cannot correct it, till Mr C has finally done with it." Brewer MS, Murray to [Croker], June 3 [1811]: ". . . I went to the Admiralty and saw there Mr Barrow . . . as I could not ascertain anything respecting a packet which I had sent on Saturday afternoon containing Pasley, I have thought it better to send you another Copy . . ." Brightfield 453. See also Warter II, 209-10, 223, 228 ("great omissions and alterations"), 308; Southey 272, 274-75; Forster 155; Rickman 154; Heber I, 411

149. Article 9. Lee and Girdlestone: Translations of Pindar

HEBER, REGINALD. Murray Reg. Murray MS, Gifford to Murray, [May? 1811]: "I have heard from Mr Reginald Heber this morning, he promises

Pindar this week." Murray MS, Gifford to Murray, [May 1811]: "Mr Heber wishes to see the proof of Pindar." Murray MS, Gifford to Murray, [May 1811]: "I . . . send back Pindar . . . in hopes that you may be able to send it to Hodnet Hall . . ." [Hodnet Hall was the home of Heber]. Murray MS, Gifford to Murray, [May 1811]: "Pindar is arrived . . . it wants perhaps an extract or two." Heber I, 350 and note. *Gentleman's* XXI, 138

150. Article 10. Reflections on the License Trade

? ELLIS, GEORGE. Murray MS, Gifford to Murray, [May 1811]: "Pray send Mr E the pamphlet for it is a subject much canvassed—Mr C thinks that a 'Licenses' will be important."

151. Article 11. Mrs Tighe's Psyche

HEBER, REGINALD. Murray Reg. Cites Murray's marked *QR*

152. Article 12. Baron Von Sach's Voyage to Surinam

Author not identified

153. Article 13. Letters of Madame du Deffand etc.

GRANT, CHARLES, and CROKER, JOHN WILSON. Murray Reg.: "Chas Grant." Addit. note: "Aided by Croker." Cites Murray's marked *QR*. Murray MS, Gifford to Murray, [Jany 1810]: "Should not something be said to Mr Croker about the translation of Deffand? Murray MS, Gifford to Murray, [1811]: "If you have not sent Madame du Deffand to Sunning Hill, pray send it to me, as I shall be able to find a good writer for it." Murray MS, Gifford to Murray, [June 12, 1811]: "Deffand I have not heard of—nor is Girdleston [see Entry 149] come back, though— M—H [i.e., Mr Heber?] expects it some time today." Brightfield 453. *DNB*: Grant. *Gentleman's* XXI, 138: Croker

Volume VI, Number 11 (August 1811)
Published in October: Murray Reg.

154. Article 1. Stewart's Philosophical Essays

NAPIER, MACVEY. Murray Reg.: "Archdeacon Lyall." Addit. note: "Mr Napier in his life of his father—Macvey Napier attributes this article to him [i.e. Napier]." Napier 3-5 and note. Smiles I, 194. *DNB*. *See also* Robberds II, 383-84

LYALL, WILLIAM ROWE. Murray Reg.: "Archdeacon Lyall." Addit. note: "Mr Napier in his life of his father—Macvey Napier attributes this article to him [i.e. Napier]." *DNB*

? BOWDLER, JOHN THE YOUNGER. *Gentleman's* XXI, 138: Bowdler?

155. Article 2. Sarrazin's Confession du Général Buonaparté

ELLIS, GEORGE. Murray Reg.: "George Ellis." Addit. note: "See W G's letter May 28, 1811. Also Aug 4 'before it is worked off I will show it to Mr C'[anning]." Murray MS, Gifford to Murray, [May 28, 1811]: "I saw Mr G Ellis yesterday—he has nearly finished Sarazin." Murray MS, Gifford to Murray, Aug 4, 1811: "Mr Ellis will, or probably has already made a few alterations in Sarrazin: but before it is worked off, I shall show it to Mr C . . ." Murray MS, Gifford to Murray, [Sept 1811]. "Mr — has seen Sarazin . . . recommends a transposition in p. 38. I think it will improve it & . . . it should be made—as well as one small ommission on p. 25 another on p. 38. . ." Brewer MS, Murray to [Croker], n.d.: ". . . we have put in the article on Sarazin this time modified . . ."

156. Article 3. Milner's Ecclesiastical Architecture

WHITAKER, THOMAS DUNHAM. Murray Reg. Murray MS, Gifford
to Murray, Aug 4, 1811: "Milner must by all means, be sent immediately
to Dr Whitaker. It requires, I see, some revision, Townson, if printed,
should go at the same time. . ." Nichols xxix.

157. Article 4. Cuthbert's New Theory of the Tides

YOUNG, THOMAS. Murray Reg. Brande XXVIII, 157. *Gentleman's* XXI,
138. Young 157, 435. Pettigrew IV, 21

158. Article 5. Chalmers's History of the University of Oxford

? COPLESTON, EDWARD. Murray Reg.: "?Coplestone" in pencil. Addit.
note: "Coplestone wrote in this No. See W G Aug 4/11. . ." Murray MS,
Gifford to Murray, Aug 4, 1811: "I will write to Mr Davidson, & Mr
Copleston by this post." Murray MS, Gifford to Murray, [Sept 1811]:
". . . nothing is arrived from Oxford."

159. Article 6. Churton's Works of Rev R Townson

WHITAKER, THOMAS DUNHAM. Murray Reg.: "? Dr Whitaker."
Addit. note: "See W G's letter Aug 4, 1811." Murray MS, Gifford to
Murray, Aug 4, 1811: "Milner must by all means, be sent immediately to
Dr Whitaker. It requires, I see, some revision. Townson, if printed, should
go at the the same time. . ." Nichols xxix.

160. Article 7. Wilks's Sketches of the South of India

BARROW, JOHN. Murray Reg. Murray MS, Gifford to Murray, [Oct 9,
1811]: "I wrote Barrow about the Teapot . . . I do not like the word."
Murray MS, Gifford to Murray, [by Oct 1811]: "Mr B likes his Article
. . . thinks I have omitted too much of his quotation . . . the Dr [Ireland ?]
who has seen one part of it, is much pleased. These letters may refer to
Entry 165.

161. Article 8. Hardy's Life of Earl Charlemont

DUDLEY, JOHN WILLIAM WARD, LORD. Murray Reg. Kern &
Schneider in *PMLA* LX, 176. *Gentleman's* XXI, 138. *QR* LVII, 323

162. Article 9. Mathison's Notices Respecting Jamaica

ELLIS, GEORGE. Murray Reg. Murray MS, Gifford to Murray, [Sept
1811]: "I send back also Mr E which should please [follow ?] Charlemont
[Entry 161]. . . ." Murray MS, Gifford to Murray, [Oct 1811]: "I send
the remainder of Hardy [Entry 161] & the beginning of Jamaica."

163. Article 10. Edgeworth's Essays on Professional Education

DAVISON, JOHN. Murray Reg. Murray MS, Gifford to Murray, Aug
4, 1811: "I will write to Dr Davidson, & Mr Copleston by this post." Murray MS, Gifford to Murray, [Oct 1811]: "The next proof to this containing
Jamaica [Entry 162] & the beginning of Davidson is also ready . . ." *Gentleman's* XXI, 138. *DNB*

164. Article 11. Bishop of Lincoln's Refutation of Calvinism

D'OYLY, GEORGE, and GIFFORD, WILLIAM. Murray Reg.: "? Dr
D'Oyly Oxford" in pencil. Addit. note: ". . . Dr D'Oyly [wrote in this
No. of QR] See No 141-142." Murray MS, Gifford to Murray, [Sept 1811,
numbered 141]: "I send . . . the Review of India. D'Oyly article, I think,
came next. . ." Murray MS, Gifford to Murray, [Sept 1811, numbered
142]: "Do not form your opinion of D'Oyly till he is set up & seen together . . . I have taken great pains & shall yet do more . . . Davidson,
however, must come first. After this, Dr D, I suppose, Infanticide [Entry
165]." Notation on letter: "Bishop of Lincoln." Murray MS, Gifford to

Murray, n.d.: "If you mean—by being no Calvinist that D'Oyly is not to come in, I do not see how this can be." Murray MS, Gifford to Murray, [Oct 9, 1811]: "There are two passages in D'Oyly . . . which I wish much to omit." Murray MS, Gifford to Murray, [Oct 1811]: "I send D'Oyly which I have improved—" *See also* Smiles I, 203

165. Article 12. Moor's Hindu Infanticide

BARROW, JOHN. Murray Reg. The Murray MS letters quoted in Entry 160 may refer to this article

166. Article 13. Scott's Vision of Don Roderick

? ERSKINE, WILLIAM. Murray Reg.: "? Mr Erskine." Addit. note: "See W G's letters 152 & 153." Murray MS, Gifford to Murray, Aug 4, 1811: "Mr Heber has declined Scott, and Mr G Ellis rather wishes to do the same . . . I think some one may be found. . ." Murray MS, Gifford to Murray, [Oct 1811, numbered 152]: ". . . say *not one word* to any soul about the writer of Scott's review. . ." Murray MS, Gifford to Murray, [Oct 1811, numbered 153]: "I want the proof of Scott's poem, the moment it can be got ready—I am now writing to Scott & to Mr Erskine." Murray MS, Gifford to Murray, [Oct 9, 1811]: "I think it hardly necessary to send the proof to Scott." Graham 41: William Erskine?

167. Article 14. Faber's Internal State of France

CROKER, JOHN WILSON. Murray Reg. Murray MS, Gifford to Murray, [May 28, 1811]: "I shall see Mr Croker tomorrow. It is he that is to take Faber?" Brewer MS, Murray to [Croker], n.d.: "I have just seen Mr Gifford who has given me the new portion of Faber which I have sent to the printer . . . we have put in the article on Sarazin this time modified —so that the more excursive Faber is made the more it [will] be improved." Brewer MS, Murray to [Croker], June 3, [1811]: "We are grateful for your obliging attention to Faber which will be set up immediately." Murray MS, Gifford to Murray, Aug 4, 1811: "I intend to write this morning to Mr Croker about Faber; if it goes on as it begins, it will be an excellent article . . ." Murray MS, Gifford to Murray, n.d.: "Mr Croker asks about the notice of the translation of Faber." Murray MS, Gifford to Murray, [Oct 1811]: ". . . I think we must . . . put in Faber—which I will reduce & make very readable. I fear Mr Croker may be hurt and we must keep him in good humour . . ." Jennings I, 314-15 and note. Brightfield 453

168. Article 15. Bell and Lancaster's Systems of Education

SOUTHEY, ROBERT, and GIFFORD, WILLIAM. Murray Reg.: "R Southey." Murray MS, Gifford to Murray, [October 9, 1811]: "I send you the remainder of Southey . . . great care must be taken to see that the last page be properly filled up from my corrected proof." Murray MS, Gifford to Murray, [October 18, 1811]: ". . . I have taken fright upon reading over the last sheet. I am quite afraid at Southey's violence and must leave out the passages which attack the E R so personally. I am sure Mr Ellis would be displeased. . . We must not . . . enter into our friend Southey's quarrel." Notation on letter: "Bell & Lancaster." Murray MS, Gifford to Murray, [October 18, 1811]: ". . . I am alarmed at the danger we ran— I am quite sure we should have terrified our best friends. . . Pray do not let a line of the last sheet go out, I have desired Rowarth's boy to call at half past 8 by which time all the omissions will be made." Notation on letter: "Bell & Lancaster." Murray MS, Gifford to Murray, [October 18, 1811]: ". . . I hope that I have made Southey now safe & am confident that I have taken no part of his spirit or meaning from him. I was doubtful of the king & princess [Prince?] for the king unluckily supported Lancaster, & of the prince I knew nothing—Nor do I quite believe what he said of the ministers—for Percival, I rather think is not so warm as he fancies. He is now safe." Notation on letter: "Bell & Lancaster." British

Museum MS, Southey to Danvers, Oct 24, 1811: "Dr Bell is also at Keswick. I have been fighting his battles in the Quarterly, & had not my work been mutilated even more unmercifully than usual, this essay would have been the severest blow that the Edinburgh Review ever received. . ." Robberds II, 348: "All the stings . . . drawn." Southey 577 and 278: "all the shot of my heavy artillery . . . drawn before the guns were fired." Cottle 242-43. Warter II, 248, 250, 298. *CHEL* XIV, 449. *CBEL* III, 107. *See also* Southey 278; Warter II, 236

Volume VI, Number 12 (December 1811)

Published after January 26, 1812: from Murray's notation on Gifford's MS letter. But *see* Smiles I, 198

169. Article 1. Tracts on Spanish and Portugueze Inquisitions

SOUTHEY, ROBERT. Murray Reg. British Museum MS, Southey to Peachey, Feb. 13, 1812: "The last Quarterly has two excellent articles by Barrow upon the Russian circumnavigation, & our Eastern conquests. Those upon Montgomery & the Inquisition are mine." British Museum MS, Southey to Danvers, May 9, 1812: "There was an article of mine in the last Quarterly upon the Inquisition containing a good deal of knowledge which probably no other person in this country possessed, collected in great part from Portuguese manuscripts." Warter II, 251 and 267. Cottle 242-43. Southey 577. *See also* Warter II, 236; Smiles I, 198

170. Article 2. Krusenstern's Russian Embassy to Japan

BARROW, JOHN. Murray Reg. Addit. note: "W G's letter Nov 26/11 & Jan 26/12 'B's review was made from the Mss of Hoppner.'" Murray MS, Gifford to Murray, [Nov 26, 1811]: "Barrow has contrived to make out a most excellent article out of Krusenstern. . ." Murray MS, Gifford to Murray, [Dec 6, 1811]: "I send . . . more of Barrow's amusing article." Notation on letter identifies Krusenstern. Murray MS, Gifford to Murray, [Jany 26, 1812]: "I send a chapter of Krusenstern—The pencil marks are not meant for any thing. They were merely made by Mr B to mark the progress of translation." Notation on letter, after "Mr B": "Barrow whose Review was made from the mss of Hoppner." British Museum Ms, Southey to Peachey, Feb 13, 1812: see Entry 169. *See also* Smiles I, 198

171. Article 3. Courayer sur la Divinité de Jesus Christ

IRELAND, JOHN. Murray Reg.: "Dr Ireland?" Addit. note: "See W G's letters Dec 24/11 & Jan 3/12." Murray MS, Gifford to Murray, [Dec 24, 1811]: "You have . . . the article of Russia, carefully corrected except about 8 or ten lines which begin the sheet containing the Drs article, & which I am now correcting." Murray MS, Gifford to Murray, [Jany 3, 1813]: "I want Dr Ireland's revise"

172. Article 4. Montgomery's Poems

SOUTHEY, ROBERT. Murray Reg. British Museum MS, Southey to Peachey, Feb 13, 1812: see Entry 169. Warter II, 251. Cottle 242-43. Southey 577. *Gentleman's* XXI, 138. Graham 41. *See also* Smiles I, 198; Warter II, 242, 258

173. Article 5. Ensor on National Education

COPLESTON, EDWARD. Copleston 347

CANNING, GEORGE. Murray Reg. *Gentleman's* XXI, 138. *See also* Smiles I, 198

174. Article 6. Baron Smith on Competency of Witnesses
    CROKER, JOHN WILSON. Murray Reg. Brightfield 453. *See also* Smiles
    I, 198

175. Article 7. Hoare's Ancient Wiltshire, Part II
    WHITAKER, THOMAS DUNHAM. Murray Reg. Murray MS, Gifford
    to Murray, [Nov 26, 1811]: "Whitaker has sent an article on Stonehenge—
    sober & judicious." Nichols xxix.

176. Article 8. Buchanan's Christian Researches in Asia
    WHITAKER, THOMAS DUNHAM. Nichols xxix.
    ? SUMNER, JOHN BIRD. Murray Reg.: "? J B Sumner." Addit. note:
    "? Mr Turners [Sumner's?] art. on this seems to have been forstalled &
    declined. See W G's Jany 26/12. See Mr Sumners letter Dec 20 1811."
    Murray MS, Gifford to Murray, [Jany 26, 1812]: "You shall have your
    letter tomorrow." Notation on letter: "To Mr Turner [Sumner?]—an ex-
    cuse for not using his article on Buchanans Xtian Researches."

177. Article 9. Ford's Dramatic Works, by Weber; Gilchrist's Letter to Gifford
    GIFFORD, WILLIAM, and FIELD, BARRON. Murray Reg.: "Barron
    Field. in fact W Gifford." Murray MS, Gifford to Murray, n.d.: "I have
    lost Gilchrist's letter & do not recollect to whom—pray send me a copy . . .
    & I will then complete the Article." Murray MS, Gifford to Murray, [Jany
    8, 1812]: "Certainly what I have is curious—and I can make the other
    sheet good . . ." Notation on letter: "Weber Ford Plays." Murray MS,
    Gifford to Murray, [Jany 18, 1812]: "Mr C is already as [?] is the re-
    vision of Ford." Morgan MS, Southey to [Moxon], July 19, 1837: Gif-
    ford's calling Lamb insane in *QR* was not intentional. Smiles I, 200-1
    GIFFORD, WILLIAM. *Gentleman's* XXI, 138. Graham 41. Graham in *SP*
    XXII, 508. Clark 156 and note; 190-91; 222-23; Pfeiffer in *PQ* XI, 411.
    See also Southey 417 note; Robinson I, 62-63; Clark 187 and 273 note
    98; *QR* CCX, 759

178. Article 10. Java and Its Dependencies
    BARROW, JOHN. Murray Reg.: "J Barrow." Addit. note: "See W G's
    letters Jany 3/12 & Jany 5/12" Murray MS, Gifford to Murray, [Jany
    24, 1812]: "I sent you the residue of Barrow of which I fear I shall not
    receive a line, till the whole be before the great men . . ." Notation by
    Murray II on letter: "Mr Yorke and Mr Percival, who were very much
    afraid that they had allowed Mr Barrow to say too much respecting the
    future intervention of Government, in regard to their late conquest of Java,
    in Mr Barrow's article upon that subject. The sheets were however re-
    turned on Sunday Jan 26th without any important change." Barrow's au-
    thorship is indubitable: 11 other MS letters from Gifford to Murray bear
    upon it, 7 of them annotated. British Museum MS, Southey to Peachey,
    Feb 13, 1812: see Entry 169. Smiles I, 198-99

179. Article 11. Trotter's Memoirs of Charles James Fox
    CANNING, GEORGE, and ELLIS, GEORGE. Murray Reg.: "Geo Can-
    ning? & G Ellis." Addit. note: "W G's letter Jan 1, 1812." Murray MS,
    Gifford to Murray [Jany 1, 1812]: "Nothing is come today—but we need
    not fear, as they are at work." Notation on letter: "Mr C & G E on Trot-
    ters Fox & Cannings speech." Murray MS, Gifford to Murray, [Jany 6,
    1812]: ". . . Trotter . . . will be most excellent . . . Mr C is . . . at Mr
    C Ellis's . . . send the whole there. . . [C goes soon to Sunning Hill,
    where] the Article will be completed on Saturday . . ." Murray MS, Gif-
    ford to Murray, [Jany 20, 1812]: "Trotter . . . I thought it right . . . to
    say a word of Pitt, & therefore sent to our friend at 1200 oclock to put
    something in . . ." Murray MS, Gifford to Murray, [Jany 20, 1812]: "Mr
    ———is now with me & has brought what I wished." Notation on letter:
    "Sketch of character of Pitt in Trotter's Life of Fox Canning." Murray MS,

Gifford to Murray, [Jany 24, 1812]: "I shall have the revise from Mr Canning today..." Notation on letter: "Trotter's Mem. Fox." Murray MS, Gifford to Murray, [Jany 26, 1812]: "The last, of course, you will not print off till it returns from Mr C." Notation on letter: "Canning—3 pages Trotter affixed to above." Seven other MS letters from Gifford to Murray (6 of them annotated) bear upon authorship: none of them specific about Ellis. Marriott 146: "by Canning (perhaps assisted by Ellis)." Smiles I, 199

FRERE, JOHN HOOKHAM. *Gentleman's* XXI, 138

Volume VII, Number 13 (March 1812)
Published after May 9, 1812: see Warter II, 267

180. Article 1. America—Orders in Council

BARROW, JOHN, and GIFFORD, WILLIAM. Murray Reg.: "J Barrow." Murray MS, Gifford to Murray, [Dec 7, 1811]: "... I sent to Mr Cr [Croker] as I promised. Mr C—[Canning] has written to G E [George Ellis] and I think we may expect something there ..." Notation on letter: "About an article on American affair of Lille Belt suggested by J. M." Murray MS, Gifford to Murray, [1812]: "I will not close my eyes till the whole of America is finished ... Our friend B. [Barrow] proves a tougher piece of work than I expected. ... I find some difficulty to preserve the chain of the argument clear & unbroken." Murray MS, Gifford to Murray, [March 21, 1812]: "I am glad to receive the slips & shall send them to B tomorrow." Notation on letter: "Article on America B—W—[Barrow]" *See also* Smiles I, 201

181. Article 2. Life of Bishop Porteus

WHITAKER, THOMAS DUNHAM. Murray Reg. Murray MS, Gifford to Murray, [April 20, 1812]: "I have recd the proof from Whitaker ... he has not taste enough to strike out anything ..."

182. Article 3. Mackenzie's Travels in Iceland

SOUTHEY, ROBERT. Murray Reg.: "J Barrow." Addit. note: "Southey wrote in this No See W G's letter 182." Murray MS, Gifford to Murray, [Apr 20, 1812, numbered 192]: "I send the remr of Southey. . ." British Museum MS, Southey to Danvers, May 9, 1812: "The next number [of QR] will contain a reviewal of the Iceland Traveler." British Museum MS, Southey to Peachey, April 6, 1825: "The paper in Q R no 13 upon some Travels in India is not mine ... There is a paper of mine upon Iceland in that number." Cottle 242-243. Southey 577. *See also* Warter II, 251, 267

BARROW, JOHN. Murray Reg. *See also* Smiles I, 201

183. Article 4. Lingard's Antiquities of the Saxon Church

WHITAKER, THOMAS DUNHAM. Nichols xxix

184. Article 5. Cooke's History of Reformation in Scotland

? SCOTT, WALTER. Murray Reg.: "? Sir W Scott" in pencil. Addit. note in pencil: "This suggestion is derived from Giffords letter to Scott, lent to me by D Douglas July 1893." Murray MS, Gifford to Murray, [April 1812]: "Nothing from Sunning Hill—nor from Scott."

185. Article 6. Haafner's Travels in India

BARROW, JOHN. Murray Reg. Addit. note: "See W G's letter Mar 14/12." Murray MS, Gifford to Murray, [April 1812]: "Barrow ... wishes much for an Article on India ..." *See also* Smiles I, 201

186. Article 7. Biot's Traite Elémentaire d'Astronomie Physique
    YOUNG, THOMAS. Murray Reg.

187. Article 8. Portugal: A Poem by Lord Grenville
    CROKER, JOHN WILSON. Murray Reg. Murray MS, Gifford to Murray,
    [Apr 1812]: "Barrow suggests something on Portugal for our next, but
    I know not whether he can get it done." Murray MS, Gifford to Murray,
    [Apr 24, 1812]: "I send you Mr C cut down to a very pleasant article."
    Brightfield 454

188. Article 9. Romilly on Criminal Law
    DAVISON, JOHN. Murray Reg. *Gentleman's* XXI, 138. *D N B*

189. Article 10. Byron's *Childe Harold* I and II
    ELLIS, GEORGE. Murray Reg. Murray MS, Gifford to Murray, [Nov
    1811]: "I like Lord B's letter, & will send it to G E . . . something may
    be done perhaps . . . say as little as possible . . . till we hear from Sunning
    Hill." Murray MS, Gifford to Murray, [1812]: ". . . Child Harold . . .
    must not go *without* the extracts, for those Mr E *expressly* desires may be
    inserted." Smiles I, 126. *Gentleman's* XXI, 138. Graham 41. *C B E L*
    III, 192

190. Article 11. Sir John Nicoll on Lay Baptism
    PHILLPOTTS, HENRY. Murray Reg.: "Rev H Phillpotts." Addit. note:
    "The Bp of Exeter's first contribution to Q R, he was introduced by Cople-
    stone." Cites Murray's marked *QR*. Smiles I, 201
    ? HEBER, REGINALD. *Gentleman's* XXI, 139: "supposed to be written by
    Bp Heber."

Volume VII, Number 14 (June 1812)
Published between July 10 and August 14: Murray MS, Gifford to Murray;
and Southey 286

191. Article 1. Walton's Present State of the Spanish Colonies
    WHITE, JOSEPH BLANCO. Murray Reg.: "Wm Jacob." Addit. note in
    pencil near Art 9: "Blanco White wrote in this art. See W G's letters Nos
    197-98." [That Addit. note confused Barrow's South American article,
    Entry 199, with White's.] Murray MS, Gifford to Murray, [July 4, 1812,
    numbered 197]: "I must add something to Blanco, to bring him down to
    the present day." Murray MS, Gifford to Murray, [July 6, 1812, numbered
    198]: "Blanco second sheet I have not yet done with . . . [Though the Ar-
    ticle is good,] the language . . . is a Spaniards." Thom III, 468. *See also*
    Southey 280
    JACOB, WILLIAM. Murray Reg. But *see* evidence above, under White

192. Article 2. Roscoe's Letters on Reform
    DUDLEY, JOHN WILLIAM WARD, LORD. Murray Reg. Smiles I,
    202. *QR* LXVII, 97. *Gentleman's* XXI, 139

193. Article 3. Jones's ed. of Baker's Biographia Dramatica
    GILCHRIST, OCTAVIUS GRAHAM, and GIFFORD, WILLIAM. Mur-
    ray MS, Gifford to Murray, [Feb 26, 1812]: "Gilchrist . . . is much pleased
    with the Art. in hand." Murray MS, Gifford to Murray, [possibly mis-
    dated March 14, 1812]: "Gilchrist has almost finished Jones (?) he says
    . . ." Murray MS, Gifford to Murray, [Oct 6, 1812]: "As to the Reply . . . it
    is absolute perfection . . . If there be a halter in Stamford we shall hear
    no more of poor Gilchrist . . . Mr Barrow will frank a copy for you to

Gilchrist." Notation on letter: "Jones's pamphlet on QR." *D N B*: Gilchrist. Graham 41: Gilchrist. Clark 194: ". . . much like Gifford's work . . . There is the possibility that Gifford only added to Gilchrist's article."

GIFFORD, WILLIAM, and FIELD, BARRON. Murray Reg.: "Barron Field but mainly W. Gifford."

194. Article 4. Dr Eveleigh's Sermons

? D'OYLY, GEORGE. Murray Reg.: "Dr D'oyly." Addit. note: "? Dr Ireland see W G July 4, 1812." Murray MS, Gifford to Murray, [July 4, 1812]: "Whatever be the case, Eveleigh cannot be left out this time without displeasing Dr Ireland, who fully expects it." Murray MS, Gifford to Murray, postmarked July 10, [1812]: "Eveleigh, I have cut down into a very unexceptionable article . . ." *See also* Smiles I, 203

? IRELAND, JOHN. See evidence above, under D'Oyly

195. Article 5. Galt's Voyages and Travels

? FERRIAR, JOHN. Murray Reg.: "? Dr Ferriar" in pencil

196. Article 6. Mrs Barbauld's 1811: A Poem

CROKER, JOHN WILSON. Murray Reg. Brewer MS, Murray to [Croker], [pencil notation: 1812]: Murray recommends mercy, instead of the sweeping severity in the closing paragraph of the article on Mrs Barbauld; except for those last sentences, he considers the article particularly lively and happy. Graham 41. Clark 197; 271 note 28. Brightfield 454. *See also* Smiles I, 202

197. Article 7. Reid's Life of Horne Tooke

DUDLEY, JOHN WILLIAM WARD, LORD, and COPLESTON, EDWARD. Murray Reg. *QR* LXVII, 97. *Gentleman's* XXI, 139: Dudley. Dudley-Ivy 113, note: Dudley. *DNB*: Dudley. *See also* Smiles I, 218

198. Article 8. Maria Edgeworth's Tales of Fashionable Life (Vols 4, 5, 6)

CROKER, JOHN WILSON. Murray Reg. Brewer MS, Murray to Croker, n.d.: ". . . perhaps you will make an effort upon Miss Edgeworth who merits all your care . . . we used [her] very scurvily in our Review (see no 3 or Vol 2 p 146) of the first three Vols of her Tales . . . I am very anxious for a good Article upon these Tales." Murray MS, Gifford to Murray, n.d.: "I send Edgeworth which I have been able to look at . . . we must not go too fast for ou[r fri]end." Murray MS, Gifford to Murray, [July 1812]: "Edgeworth I returned by the boy for press—having made no alteration of importance in it." Brewer MS, Murray to [Croker], n.d.: "I send the close of the admirable article with which you have favoured us upon Miss Edgewworth & for which I feel greatly obliged." Smiles I, 202. Graham 41. Brightfield 338, 454. Pfeiffer in *PQ* XI, 101-3 and notes. *C B E L* III, 368. *See also* Dudley 13-14

GIFFORD, WILLIAM. *Gentleman's* XXI, 139

199. Article 9. Mawe's Travels in Brazil

BARROW, JOHN. Murray Reg.: "J Barrow." Addit. note: "See W G's letter July 10/12." Another Addit. note, in pencil: "Blanco White wrote in this art. See W G's letters Nos 197-198." [That second Addit. note confused White's South American article, Entry 191, with Barrow's.] Murray MS, Gifford to Murray, postmarked July 10, [1812]: "Mr B has sent the first part of Mawe . . ."

200. Article 10. Sismondi's Républiques Italiennes

? MERIVALE, JOHN HERMAN. Murray Reg.: "H Merivale?" Cites Murray's marked *QR*. Murray MS, Gifford to Murray, Aug 21, 1812: "Mr Merivale, I believe, is out of town—however, they will tell you where to find him."

201. Article 11. Moore's Irish Melodies

TWISS, HORACE. Murray Reg. Murray MS, Gifford to Murray, [Apr 20, 1812]: "Pray let one of your people leave the enclosed for Mr Moore at the Temple . . ." Murray MS, Gifford to Murray, [July 6, 1812]: "Have the goodness to let one of your people take the inclosed to Mr Moore at the Temple." Graham 41
? MOORE, THOMAS. Sharpe II, 37-38: "written by himself, perhaps . . ."

202. Article 12. Hurd's Warburton's Works

WHITAKER, THOMAS DUNHAM. Murray Reg. Murray MS, Gifford to Murray, [July 6, 1812]: "I have recd the end of Whitaker's art. but unluckily the part which he is labouring at, I suppose, the Descent of Aeneas into Hell, is not arrived; he promises it directly." [See *QR* VII, 401]. *Gentleman's* XXI, 139. Graham 41. Nichols xxix

203. Article 13. Carr's Travels in Spain

CROKER, JOHN WILSON. Murray Reg. Cites unspecified old letters. Brightfield 454. *See also* Smiles I, 202

204. Article 14. Lives of the French Revolutionists

SOUTHEY, ROBERT. Murray Reg. Cites unspecified old letters. British Museum MS, Southey to Danvers, June 4, 1812: "I shall finish the Register by the end of next week, & shall require a fortnight after it for the Quarterly. Then I am ready to strap on my knapsack & start . . ." Smiles I, 202. Cottle 242-43. Southey 577, and 286: "a good deal worse for the mutilation . . ." *See also* Warter II, 251; Southey 283, 284, 285

205. Article 15. Spenser's Poems

Author not identified. Murray MS, Gifford to Murray, [July 1812]: "Spenser —I am sorry to say—I am almost afraid of. It is but feeble & will do us little good—However, I will look at it again."

206. Article 16. Markland's Euripidis Supplices

ELMSLEY, PETER. Murray Reg. Murray MS, Gifford to Murray, [July 1812]: "Greek, I think, must come last, as Elmsley says that he has an addition to make." A year later, when Elmsley applied for permission to reprint his essay, Gifford wrote the following polite refusal, which he suggested that Murray copy and send. Murray MS, Gifford to Murray, [July 7, 1813]: "I should have pleasure in complying with your [Elmsley's] wishes respecting the Article in the fourteenth No of the Q Review . . . but ... I ... fear to afford a precedent which might lead to unforseen consequences." *Gentleman's* XXI, 139

Volume VIII, Number 15 (September 1812)

Published after Nov 26, 1812, Murray MS, Gifford to Murray; and before January 5, 1813, British Museum MS, Southey to Danvers

207. Article 1. Report on National Education

CANNING, GEORGE. *Gentleman's* XXI, 139

208. Article 2. Pering and Money on Shipbuilding

BARROW, JOHN. Murray Reg. Murray MS, Gifford to Murray, Aug 21, 1821: "Mr Barrows article on ship building will be highly valuable. He is now about it." Murray MS, Gifford to Murray, [Sept 21, 1812]: "Mr Barrow has sent his Art on Shipbuilding . . ." Murray MS, Gifford to

Murray, [Oct 6, 1812]: "I send you plenty of Ship-building . . . Mr Barrow means to shew his Art to some of the old Admirals . . ." Murray MS, Gifford to Murray, [Nov 26, 1812]: "Barrow's single article on Shipbuilding is worth the whole [of *British Review*, No. 7] ten times told." Smiles, I, 284 note

209. Article 3. Specimens of a New Translation of Juvenal

GIFFORD, WILLIAM. Murray Reg.

210. Article 4. Davy's Chemical Philosophy

YOUNG, THOMAS. Murray Reg. Brande XXVIII, 157. *Gentleman's* XXI, 139. Pettigrew IV, 21

211. Article 5. Landor's Count Julian: A Tragedy

SOUTHEY, ROBERT. Murray Reg. British Museum MS, Southey to Danvers, Jany 5, 1813: "In the last Quarterly I reviewed Landor's Play, & the Calamities of Authors, but as the number has not reached me I cannot say whether [the articles] stand as they were written." Cottle 242-43. Southey 577. Forster 214: "Gifford . . . knocked its brains out . . ." Graham 41. Clark 235

212. Article 6. D'Israeli's Calamities of Authors

SOUTHEY, ROBERT. Murray Reg. British Museum MS, Southey to Danvers, Jany 5, 1813: see Entry 211. British Museum MS, Southey to Peachey, Jany 22, 1813: "In the last number I reviewed the Calamities of Authors." Cottle 242-43. Southey 291 and 577. Graham 41. *CHEL* XII, 405 and note. *See also* Smiles I, 214, 237: Grierson III, 135 and note

213. Article 7. Macpherson's European Commerce with India

ELLIS, GEORGE. Murray Reg. Cites unspecified old letters

214. Article 8. Colman's Poetical Vagaries

CROKER, JOHN WILSON. Murray Reg. Brewer MS, Murray to [Croker], n.d.: "The facetious Mr Coleman has written against us a poem with notes [see Entry 249]. Seeing that your criticisms excite so much attention—I wish you would extend them." Graham 41. Clark 68 and note. Brightfield 454

215. Article 9. Playfair's Outlines of Natural Philosophy

YOUNG, THOMAS. Murray Reg.

216. Article 10. Galt's Life of Cardinal Wolsey

WHITAKER, THOMAS DUNHAM. Murray Reg. Addit. note: "W G's letter (No 205)" Murray MS, Gifford to Murray, [Oct 1812, numbered 205]: "Dr Whitaker has just sent Galt. . ." Nichols xxix

217. Article 11. Horace and James Smith's Rejected Addresses

CROKER, JOHN WILSON. Murray Reg. Cites unspecified old letters. Brewer MS, Murray to Croker, n.d.: "I will send you tomorrow duplicate proofs of The Rejected addresses, one to correct & to forward to Mr G— & one to retain . . ." Graham 41. Clark 229. Brightfield 454. *See also* Smiles I, 218

218. Article 12. Essay on the Life and Character of Petrarch

PENROSE, JOHN. Murray Reg.: "Rev Penrose." Addit. note: "Mr P. was a friend of Ld Egremont." Cites Murray's marked *QR*
? SCOTT, WALTER. Kern in *MLQ* VI, 327-28. *See also* Grierson II, 410

219. Article 13. Mr Madison's War

BARROW, JOHN. Murray Reg.: "J Barrow?" Cites Murray's marked *QR*.

Murray MS, Gifford to Murray, [Sept 21, 1812]: "Mr Barrow . . . means to go to work—at least I hope so, on an excellent American pamphlet which the Consul has just sent to the Admiralty." Murray MS, Gifford to Murray, Nov 26, 1812: "America is returned—with nothing altered but the conclusion—except what B w himself has done."

220. Article 14. Monk's Euripidis Hippolytus

ELMSLEY, PETER. Murray Reg.
BLOMFIELD, CHARLES JAMES. *DNB* on Monk

Volume VIII, Number 16 (December 1812)

Published between January 25, 1813, and April 7, 1813: see Southey 291 and Robinson I, 127

221. Article 1. East India Company's Charter

Author not identified

222. Article 2. Littérature Française, 18me siècle

MERIVALE, JOHN HERMAN. Murray Reg.: "H Merivale (senior)"

223. Article 3. Last Years of Gustavus IV

HEBER, REGINALD. Murray Reg. Heber I, 369 and note. *Gentleman's* XXI, 139

224. Article 4. Inquiry into the Poor Laws: Colquhoun

SOUTHEY, ROBERT. Murray Reg. British Museum MS, Southey to Danvers, May 9, 1812: "I am going . . . to write upon the state of the Poor." British Museum MS, Southey to Danvers, January 5, 1813: "The Proofs of an essay on the State of the Poor or rather the populace lies now upon my desk,—being part of an [article?] for the next number. It is an attack upon Malthus,—upon the manufacturing system, & upon the Cobbetts & Hunts who have produced the Luddite feeling in the mob." British Museum MS, Southey to Peachey, January 22, 1813: "You will see a paper of mine in the next Quarterly upon this subject [the lower classes]. It enters into the moral & political state of the populace, & draws a faithful picture, which I shall be very sorry if any misjudging timidity should weaken or suppress." British Museum MS, Southey to Peachey, Dec 6, 1816: "It is more than four years since I distinctly pointed out the danger [of popular revolution] in the Quarterly Review (No. 16) . . ." Rickman 191: "castration . . . by Croker and Gifford" Robinson I, 127. Southey 338, 339, 577. Cottle 242-43. Warter III, 44. Southey's *Essays* I, 75-155. *Gentleman's* XXI, 139. *QR* CCX, 746. Graham 16. *See also* Warter II, 267, 283, 304; Rickman 157; Southey 283, 290, 291

225. Article 5. Mant's Bampton Lectures

Author not identified

226. Article 6. Lichtenstein's Travels in South Africa

BARROW, JOHN. Murray Reg. Murray MS, Gifford to Murray, n.d.: "Mr Barrow wishes much to get 'Lichtenstein's Travels in Southern Africa' . . ." Murray MS, Gifford to Murray, Aug 21, 1812: "He [Barrow] wants Lichtenstein & Somerville's Travels into South Africa." *Gentleman's* XXI, 139

227. Article 7. Electa Tentamina: Scholâ Regiâ Edinensi

? SOUTHEY, ROBERT. *DNB* on Pillans says: Southey

228. Article 8. Graham's Journal of a Residence in India

BARROW, JOHN. Murray Reg.

229. Article 9. Belsham's Memoirs of Lindsey

WHITAKER, THOMAS DUNHAM. Murray Reg. Addit. note: "from a letter of Dr W Dec 22 1812 & letter No 213." Murray MS, Gifford to Murray, [1813, numbered 213]: "I like the worthy Dr's Art on Belsham prodigiously." The words *The Dr* frequently stand for John Ireland. Nichols xxix

230. Article 10. Foscolo's Letters of Jacopo Ortis

ROSE, WILLIAM STEWART. Murray Reg.: "W S Rose"

231. Article 11. Campaign of the French in Russia, and Eustaphieve's Resources of Russia

CROKER, JOHN WILSON. Murray Reg.: "J W Croker." Addit. note: "See W G's Nov 16, 1812." Murray MS, Gifford to Murray, [November 16, 1812]: "I shall see Mr Croker today, and will speak about Russia, but as the important events have but taken place within these few days—perhaps it may be better to wait for a fuller article for our next." Notation on letter: "A projected article on Resources of Russia." Brightfield 454: Croker, probably with coadjutors

232. Article 12. Scott's Rokeby

ELLIS, GEORGE. Murray Reg. Smiles I, 126. Lockhart III, 253: ". . . I suppose, Ellis . . ." Graham 41

Volume IX, Number 17 (March 1813)
Published after April 25, or possibly after May 12: Murray MSS,
Gifford to Murray

233. Article 1. Natural and Political History of Malta, by Giacinto, Domeier and Eton

? BARROW, JOHN. Murray MS, Gifford to Murray, May 12, 1813. "By some accident pages 9 10 11 & 12 were left out of your parcel & I cannot send the proof to Mr B till I receive them. . . ."

234. Article 2. Horsley's Sermons

WHITAKER, THOMAS DUNHAM. Murray Reg. Addit. note: "from a letter of Dr W. Dec 22, 1812." Murray MS, Gifford to Murray, [1813]: "I like the worthy Dr's Art on Belsham [i.e. Entry 229] prodigiously. Horsley I have not yet looked at. I will send you a line for him tomorrow, which you must get franked." Nichols xxix

235. Article 3. Li Romani nella Grecia by Barzoni

ROSE, WILLIAM STEWART. Murray Reg. Cites unspecified old letters and Murray's marked *QR*

236. Article 4. Evelyn's Sylva

WHITAKER, THOMAS DUNHAM. Murray Reg. Cites unspecified old letters and Murray's marked *QR*

237. Article 5. Kinneir and Morier on Persia

? BARROW, JOHN. Murray Reg.: "J Barrow?" Cites unspecified old letters. Murray MS, Gifford to Murray, [April 25, 1813]: "Do you know whether M Barrow is in town? . . . it is now more than a week since I sent him the first part of Persia—The second part, he had on Wednesday." Pencil notation on letter: "Q R no. 17 Art 5" Murray MS, Murray to Gifford, April 25, 1813: ". . . Persia [this indistinct word could be: Peace] appears to me to be the very last thing in people's thoughts at this time and Horace Twiss the *very* last man who ought to be connected with our Review."

238. Article 6. Baron de Grimm's Corréspondence

MERIVALE, JOHN HERMAN. Murray Reg.: "H. Merivale (senr)." *Gentleman's* XXI, 139

239. Article 7. Dr Young's Introduction to Medical Literature

YOUNG, THOMAS. Murray Reg. Cites unspecified old letters and Murray's marked *QR*. Addit. note: "by the author of the book. . ." *QR* CCX, 741 note

240. Article 8. Feinaigle and Grey's Artificial Memory

HORTON, SIR ROBERT JOHN WILMOT—. Murray Reg.: "Sir Wilmot Horton." *Gentleman's* XXI, 139. *See also* Heber I, 371, 378

241. Article 9. Translations of the Comedies of Aristophanes

MITCHELL, THOMAS. Murray Reg.: "J H Frere?" Cites unspecified old letters and Murray's marked *QR*. Addit. note: ". . . doubtful." Murray MS, Gifford to Murray, [1813]: "The very devil is in our clever friend to be sure—he would go on forever—however, what he has sent is pleasant enough. It was but last night that I amused myself with reading the very Chorus which he has translated. [See *QR* IX, 159] . . . We want Frere for this. Pray send it to Rowarth [the printer] directly . . . It is odd enough that both Mitchell & Foscolo should have fallen upon the same part of Plato's Banquet—Both have translated it & it forms the most beautiful part of both their papers—yet one must be omitted. Prepare Foscolo for this—& you may truly say that had he been first, I would have omitted Mitchell—but you know that Mitchell has been lying on my table several months." *D N B*

FRERE, JOHN HOOKHAM. See evidence above, under Mitchell

242. Article 10. Clarke's Travels in Greece, Egypt, and the Holy Land

HEBER, REGINALD. Murray Reg. Murray MS, Gifford to Murray, [1813]: "Clark I have given to Mr R Heber. . ." *Gentleman's* XXI, 139. *See also* Grierson II, 482

243. Article 11. Samuel Roger's Poems

DUDLEY, JOHN WILLIAM WARD, LORD. Murray Reg.: "Hon J Ward (Ld Dudley)." Dudley-Ivy 180 and note; and 224 and note. Fitzpatrick's *Whately* I, 42. Rogers 53. *QR* LXVII, 96 and note. *Gentleman's* XXI, 139. Graham 41. Clark 237. *DNB*. *See also* Byron I, 185; Dudley-Ivy 221 and note

244. Article 12. Grant on Maintaining the Indian System

BARROW, JOHN. Murray Reg. Addit. note: "See W G's letter No. 223." Murray MS, Gifford to Murray, [1813, numbered 223]: "Mr B has not sent the rem'd of India . . . but I expect it every minute."

Volume IX, Number 18 (July 1813)
Published six weeks late: Smiles I, 262

245. Article 1. Tracts on British Fisheries

BARROW, JOHN. Murray Reg. *Gentleman's* XXI, 139

246. Article 2. Ferriar on Apparitions

ROSE, WILLIAM STEWART. Murray Reg.: "W.S. Rose." Cites unspecified old letters and Murray's marked *QR*. Murray MS, Gifford to Murray, [July 1813]: "I have enclosed for the printer Mr Rose's article." *See also* Smiles I, 243 and note

247. Article 3. Wakefield and Fox on Classical Literature

DUDLEY, JOHN WILLIAM WARD, LORD. Murray Reg. *QR* LVII, 97. *Gentleman's* XXI, 139. Allibone. *DNB. See also* Byron I, 185

248. Article 4. D'Oyly's Letters to Sir W Drummond

D'OYLY, GEORGE. Murray Reg. Cites unspecified old letters and Murray's marked *QR*. *QR,* CCX, 741

249. Article 5. Colman's Vagaries Vindicated

CROKER, JOHN WILSON. Murray Reg. Murray MS, Gifford to Murray, postmarked July [3?], 1813: "Colman I see advertized. Would you have me try to get at Mr Croker once more?—If the book be worth reviewing, he is the only person to do it, & I will write to him." Brewer MS, Murray to [Croker], n.d.: The facetious Mr Coleman has written against us a poem with notes. Seeing that your criticisms [see Entry 214] excite so much attention—I wish you would extend them. . . ." Smiles I, 262. Graham 41. Clark 68 and note. Brightfield 454

250. Article 6. Elmsley's Euripidis Heraclidae

BLOMFIELD, CHARLES JAMES. Murray Reg. Cites unspecified old letters and Murray's marked *QR*. *CHEL* XII, 526

251. Article 7. Montgalliard sur la Puissance Russe

? HAY, ROBERT WILLIAM. Murray Reg.: "? Rev [or R W?] Hay" in pencil. Addit. note: "See Gifford's letters to him." The article was certainly not by Reginald Heber: see Heber I, 373-74, 378, 384, 385

252. Article 8. Meadley's Memoirs of Dr Paley

? WHITAKER, THOMAS DUNHAM. Murray Reg.: "Whittaker (?)" Cites unspecified old letters. Murray MS, Gifford to Murray, [May 20, 1813]: "I enclose a letter . . . for Dr W [letter not distinct] . . . I have desired the Dr to look at our former Art & at the new Edition of Paley's life and if he thinks that the additions justify a new Art. I have told him that is just what we desire." Pencil notation on letter: "? Art in No. 18 on Paley by Dr Whitaker."

253. Article 9. Hutton's Mathematical and Philosophical Tracts

Author not identified

254. Article 10. M'Crie's Life of John Knox

WHITAKER, THOMAS DUNHAM. Murray Reg. Addit. note: "From a letter of Dr W's Ap 24, 1813." Nichols xxix

255. Article 11. Langsdorff's Voyage round the World

BARROW, JOHN. Murray Reg. Addit. note: "J B's letter June 10, 1812." Warter II, 395

256. Article 12. Villani's Istorie Fiorentine
Author not identified

257. Article 13. Blackall on Dropsies
YOUNG, THOMAS. Murray Reg. Brande XXVIII, 157. *Gentleman's* XXI, 139. Young 228. Pettigrew IV, 21

258. Article 14. Malcolm's Sketch of the Sikhs
? BARROW, JOHN. Murray Reg.: "? John Barrow" in pencil. Addit. note: "From an allusion in his letters May 4 & 5 1813."

259. Article 15. Scott's Bridal of Triermain
ELLIS, GEORGE. Murray Reg. Smiles I, 126. Lockhart III, 253: ". . . I suppose, Ellis . . ." *Gentleman's* XXI, 139. *QR* CCX, 747. Graham 41. *See also* Grierson III, 292

Volume X, Number 19 (October 1813)
Published between December 5 and January 29: Murray MS, Gifford to Murray, and Southey 302

260. Article I. India-built Ships and Naval Timber
BARROW, JOHN. Murray Reg. Cites Murray's marked *QR*. Smiles I, 284

261. Article 2. Mrs Montagu's Letters
? CROKER, JOHN WILSON. Murray Reg.: "J W Croker." Cites Murray's marked *QR* but then adds a question mark. *See also* Grierson II, 225, 236-37

262. Article 3. Earl Harrowby on the Curacy Bill
COPLESTON, EDWARD. Murray MS, Gifford to Murray, [August 30, 1813]: "Mr Coplestone has sent his Art. which is important, but which must stand over [for next QR, I believe." Copleston 46 and 347

263. Article 4. Baron de Grimm's Correspondance. Third series
MERIVALE, JOHN HERMAN. Murray Reg.: "H Merivale (senr)" Murray MS, Gifford to Murray, [September 21, 1813]: "I send Mr Merivale quantum—I am sorry to find that he is poor." Broughton I, 93 and note. Merivale 293. *Gentleman's* XXI, 139

264. Article 5. History of Dissenters
SOUTHEY, ROBERT. Murray Reg. Murray MS, Gifford to Murray, [Sept 21, 1813]: ". . . Southey . . . the Art must be curtailed in some parts." Robinson I, 139-40. Cottle 242-43. Southey 577, 302: " I perceived some omissions . . ." *Gentleman's* XXI, 139

265. Article 6. Bland's Greek Anthology
SUMNER, JOHN BIRD. Murray Reg. Addit. note: "See W G May 14/12 [next to last digit not clear]"

266. Article 7. Comber on National Subsistence
? ELLIS, GEORGE. Murray MS, Gifford to Murray, postmarked July [3?], 1813: "I have desired him [George Ellis, of Sunning Hill] to proceed— only giving a modern date & tone to his criticism; because the subject is really important & interesting, on account of the new Corn Bill etc." See

QR, 157, where the reviewer apologizes for reviewing a five-year-old book; however, he believes the article justified by the new House of Commons inquiry into the Corn Laws

267. Article 8. Hobhouse's Journey through Albania

BARROW, JOHN. Murray MS, Gifford to Murray, [Dec 5, 1813]: "I send you the Hobhouse freed from everything that hung in the least . . ." Broughton I, 81 and note

268. Article 9. Bread and Bulls, and the Inquisition

Author not identified

269. Article 10. Letter on the Conduct of Denmark

? and GIFFORD, WILLIAM. Murray Reg.: "? Mr Gifford." Cites unspecified old letters. Murray MS, Gifford to Murray, [Dec 5, 1813]: "The Danes comes next, I believe—if you compare what is now sent with the first proof you will find it much mended, & I think it will be liked. I have however been obliged to say a good deal (a page & half at least) on the Swedish Treaty, which seemed wanting to complete it, & to make all safe. By some accident, I have mislaid or lost pp 9 10 & 11 to which my addition was made, and shall be glad if you would send them to me . . ." Notation on letter: "? is Art 10 by Mr. Gifford."

270. Article 11. Eustace's Tour through Italy

? HEBER, REGINALD. Murray MS, Gifford to Murray, [Nov 10, 1813]: "The writer of Eustace who is well acquainted with Germany wishes to have Mad. de S[taël] if not preengaged." The article on Madame de Stael's *Germany,* in the next No. of *QR,* was by Heber: see Entry 275

271. Article 12. Adelung's General History of Language

YOUNG, THOMAS. Murray Reg. Murray MS, Gifford to Murray, [Sept 21, 1813]: "I can hint to Dr Yng [Young? or Grey?] & will. I have altered his Art. since you saw it & put it a little out of the old track. But I perfectly agree with you that these things must not be again. Dr Y thought his Art. good—but he evidently had not seen the Eclectic." Brande XXVIII, 157. *Gentleman's* XXI, 139. Young 241. Pettigrew IV, 21

Volume X, Number 20 (January 1814)
Published between March 25 and Apr 7: Murray MS, Gifford to Murray; and Dudley 25

272. Article 1. Miss Edgeworth's Patronage

DUDLEY, JOHN WILLIAM WARD, LORD. Murray Reg. Dudley-Ivy 170 and note. *QR* LXVII, 90 note, and 97: assisted by Copleston. Romilly-Edgeworth 39. *Gentleman's* XXI, 139. Graham 41. *See also* Dudley 8-9, 10, 13-14, 25; Dudley-Ivy 250

CROKER, JOHN WILSON. Pfeiffer in *PQ* XI, 102-3 and note. However, we recently examined the Brewer MS letter upon which Pfeiffer bases his statement. That MS letter's further allusions to Brougham and to Sir Robert Wilson convince us that it was written some years after the appearance of the 1814 review of *Patronage.*

273. Article 2. Broughton's Letters from a Mahratta Camp

BARROW, JOHN, and GIFFORD, WILLIAM. Murray Reg.: "J Barrow." Cites Murray's marked *QR.* Addit. note "much edited by Gifford." Murray MS, Gifford to Murray, [March 8, 1814]: "I have now made the Ma-

harattas a very readable article—it was a good deal confused at first."
Murray MS, Gifford to Murray, [March 22, 1814]: "I had taken great
pains yesterday with this India Art. which is loosely written (as to style
I mean) though full of good facts." Murray MS, Gifford to Murray,
[March 25, 1813]: ". . . B's India . . . I have softened it; but as Barrow
means to print it under his own . . . name, there is no reason why he may
not say what we cannot venture to do. I have therefore preserved his own
proof for him. . ."

274. Article 3. Byron's Giaour and Bride of Abydos

ELLIS, GEORGE. Murray Reg. Murray MS, Gifford to Murray, [March
8, 1814]: ". . . Giour . . . will require so little alteration as to occasion no
delay . . . the proof will arrive from Sunning Hill . . . I have desired to
Mr E to lose no time in his revise . . ." Smiles I, 126. *Gentleman's* XXI,
139. Graham 41. *CBEL* III, 193-94. *See also* Smiles I, 221

275. Article 4. Madame de Stael's L'Allemagne

HEBER, REGINALD. Murray Reg. Murray MS, Gifford to Murray,
[March 8, 1814]: "This moment I have rec'd the *whole* of Mad. de Stael
from Mr Reg. H. . ." Heber I, 396 and note. *Gentleman's* XXI, 139. *See
also* Smiles I, 314

276. Article 5. Butler's Lives of Bossuet and Fenelon

? SOUTHEY, ROBERT. Murray Reg: "R. Southey." Addit. note: "?
by Dr Whitaker—see his letter of Oct 27, 1813." *Gentleman's* XXI, 139:
Southey
? WHITAKER, THOMAS DUNHAM. Murray Reg.: "R Southey." Addit.
note: "? by Dr Whitaker—see his letter of Oct 27, 1813."

277. Article 6. Goethe on Colours

YOUNG, THOMAS. Murray Reg. Brande XXVIII, 157. *Gentleman's* XXI,
139. Pettigrew IV, 21

278. Article 7. Hermes—State of the Modern Greeks

WHITAKER, THOMAS DUNHAM. Murray Reg. Cites unspecified old
letters. Murray MS, Gifford to Murray, [March 8, 1814]: ". . . Whitaker
on Greece."
? CANNING, STRATFORD. Murray MS, Stanley Lane Poole to Mr John
Murray, June 14, [1887]: "I have a letter from George Canning to his
cousin, Stratford, in which he says, 'I return your proof . . . it will do
you good in Giff's credit'—dated 20 Feb 1814. The proof appears to have
dealt with matters of style of grammar for G C criticises some of Stratford's remarks about 'aorists and paulas' & the 'explosion of the dual
number.' Can this be a Quarterly article?" Notation on letter: "Ansd
15/VI/87, 1st quotn evidently refers to No 20 Art 7."

279. Article 8. Paulding's Lay of the Scottish Fiddle

CROKER, JOHN WILSON. Murray Reg. Cites unspecified old letters.
Murray MS, Gifford to Murray, [Jany 19, 1814]: "I will see in the morning what can be done with the Lay—Omission of some parts of it, perhaps." Brightfield 454. *See also* Smiles I, 244; Grierson III, 395-96

280. Article 9. Resolutions of the London Ship Owners

Author not identified

281. Article 10. Intercepted Letters, etc. to Napoleon

CROKER, JOHN WILSON. Murray Reg. Cites unspecified old letters.
Murray MS, Gifford to Murray, [Jany 19, 1814]: "I have read the Intercepted Art . . . what will be said of the politicks of it? . . . if Peace be
made it must be softened. We shall see what Mr Croker will do . . ."

Murray MS, Gifford to Murray, [March 22, 1814]: "I hope Mr Croker has not left in anything about the Bourbons at this critical time." Murray MS, Gifford to Murray, [March 25, 1814]: "About 11 last night Mr C sent his Art. It must be docked, that is, the last part, which is the only heavy part, taken off—but I will set to work immediately." Brightfield 454

282. Article 11. Ingersoll's Inchiquin's United States

BARROW, JOHN. Murray Reg. Addit. note: "From 5 letters of J B Nov 1813 *wh* show that he was then engaged on an article on America for QR." Murray MS, Gifford to Murray, [March 8, 1814]: "send me the second sheet of America . . . this [copy] I have scratched on." Graham 10
? GIFFORD, WILLIAM. Tichnor I, 58
SOUTHEY, ROBERT. British Museum Catalog, under number 1431, c. 19
HALL, BASIL. Graham in *PQ* II, 101 and note

Volume XI, Number 21 (April 1814)

Published between July 2 and July 30: Murray MS, Gifford to Murray; and Robinson I, 146

283. Article 1. Ginguené and Sismondi's Literary History of Italy

BLAND, ROBERT. Marshall 382
? SOUTHEY, ROBERT. Murray MS, Thomas Young to [Gifford], Aug 29, 1814: "I have not long had the review [i.e. *QR*, No. 21]. The Italian article has given me much pleasure. I conclude it is Southey's."

284. Article 2. Galt's Tragedies

CROKER, JOHN WILSON. Murray Reg. Cites unspecified old letters. Brightfield 454

285. Article 3. Malus, Biot, Seebeck, and Brewster on Light

YOUNG, THOMAS. Murray Reg. Brande XXVIII, 157. *Gentleman's* XXI, 139. Young 380 and note. *DNB*. Pettigrew IV, 21

286. Article 4. Letters on the Nicobar Islands

SOUTHEY, ROBERT. Cottle 242-43. Southey 577. *See also* Smiles I, 239; Southey 303
? BARROW, JOHN. Murray Reg.: "? Barrow" in pencil

287. Article 5. Nelson's Letters to Lady Hamilton

CROKER, JOHN WILSON. Murray Reg. Brightfield 454

288. Article 6. Montgomery's World Before the Flood

SOUTHEY, ROBERT, and GIFFORD, WILLIAM. Murray Reg.: "R Southey & Gifford." Murray MS, Gifford to Murray, [June 3, 1814]: "After Lord Nelson I propose Montgomery, which I will make a very readable article . . ."
SOUTHEY, ROBERT. Cottle 242-43. Southey 577. *Gentleman's* XXI, 139. Graham 41. *See also* Southey 295, 303
COLERIDGE, JOHN TAYLOR. Coleridge 210

289. Article 7. Busby's Lucretius

DRURY, [Benjamin Heath?]. Murray Reg.: "Rev R [or B?] Drury."

290. Article 8. Skioldebrand, etc. Travels through Norway, Lapland, etc.

? HAY, ROBERT WILLIAM. Murray Reg.: "? R W Hay" in pencil. Addit. note: "one of Gifford's letters to him."

291. Article 9. D'Arblay's Wanderer

CROKER, JOHN WILSON. Murray Reg. Cites unspecified old letters. Graham 41. Brightfield 454
GIFFORD, WILLIAM. Grierson III, 465 note

292. Article 10. Kirwan's Sermons

Author not identified. Murray Reg.: ". . . A friend of Mr Hebers' W G." Murray MS, Gifford to Murray, [June 3, 1814]: "A friend of Mr Hebers has sent me a short article on Dean Kirwan's Sermons . . . the Art is good."

293. Article 11. Lacretelle's Histoire de France

Author not identified

294. Article 12. S. T. Coleridge's Remorse

COLERIDGE, JOHN TAYLOR. Murray Reg.: "Judge Coleridge." Brewer MS, Murray to [Croker], n.d.: "Seeing that your [Croker's] criticisms excite so much attention—I wish you would extend them— . . . Perhaps *Remorse* would not cost you much labor. *You can depend upon secrecy.*" Graham in *PMLA* XXXVIII, 286 note 17. Graham 41

295. Article 13. History of the Azores

Author not identified

296. Article 14. Bancroft on Colours

YOUNG, THOMAS. Murray Reg. Murray MS, Gifford to Murray, [July 2, 1814]: "The enclosed is for Dr Young . . . If you happen to have a copy of his article, pray get it franked by this post to Worthing. . ." Murray MS, Thomas Young to [Gifford], Aug 29, 1814: "Murray has miscalculated the pages of one of my articles, which makes only 12—not 14." Brande XXVIII, 157. *Gentleman's* XXI, 139. Young 50-51. Pettigrew IV, 21

297. Article 15. Thames Ship-Builders

BARROW, JOHN. Murray Reg.: "? Barrow" in pencil. Murray MS, Gifford to Murray, [June 3, 1814]: "I send . . . a lively m.s. of Mr B to set up *immediately.*"

Volume XI, Number 22 (July 1814)

Published after October 20: Murray MS, Gifford to Murray

298. Article 1. Brand's Popular Antiquities

COHEN, FRANCIS. Murray Reg. Smiles I, 284-85 and note. Palgrave. *See also* Merivale 214; Young 246

299. Article 2. Russian Voyages Round the World

BARROW, JOHN. Young 246

300. Article 3. Mason's Life of Gray, ed. by Mathias

WHITAKER, THOMAS DUNHAM. Nichols xxix and xxxiv. *See also* Young 246.

301. Article 4. Davy's Agricultural Chemistry

YOUNG, THOMAS. Murray Reg. Brande XXVIII, 157. *Gentleman's* XXI, 139. Pettigrew IV, 21. *See also* Young 247.

302. Article 5. Chinese Literature in Europe

BARROW, JOHN. Young 246

303. Article 6. Adams on Diseases of the Eye

YOUNG, THOMAS. Brande XXVIII, 157. *Gentleman's* XXI, 139. Young 228 note. Pettigrew IV, 21. *See also* Young 247.

304. Article 7. Scott's Waverley

CROKER, JOHN WILSON. Murray Reg.: "J W Croker." Addit. note: "not mentioned in Mr Croker's own list." Jennings I, 84 and note. *QR* CCX, 741. Graham 41. Brightfield 454. Hillhouse 47
GIFFORD, WILLIAM. Lockhart V, 150. *Gentleman's* XXI, 139

305. Article 8. Badham's Translation of Juvenal

GIFFORD, WILLIAM. Murray Reg. Murray MS, Gifford to Murray, postmarked July 27, 1814: ". . . as you must make up a parcel, pray put up that No of the Revw which contains the revise [review?] of the specimen of a Translation of Juvenal, as I should like to take the translation in hand here. It is I believe, the 18th No [actually, No. 15; see Entry 209] . . ." Clark 195: most likely, Gifford

306. Article 9. Baron De Grimm's Correspondance Littéraire

? MERIVALE, JOHN HERMAN. Murray Reg.: "R Southey." Addit. note: "Apparently Mr Merivale had an Art in this No." Murray MS, Gifford to Murray, July 15, 1814: "I am quite sorry that I did not give you Mr Merivale's draft—he probably wants it . . . This [His?] little art. I had not the leisure to revise." *Gentleman's* XXI, 139
SOUTHEY, ROBERT. See above, under Merivale

307. Article 10. Wewitzer, School for Wits, and Kett's Flowers of Wit

? MERIVALE, JOHN HERMAN, and GIFFORD, WILLIAM. Murray Reg's. Addit. note: "Apparently Mr. Merivale had an Art in this No." Murray MS, Gifford to Murray, Ryde, July 15, 1814: "I am quite sorry that I did not give you Mr Merivale's draft—he probably wants it... This [His?] little art. I had not the leisure to revise." Murray MS, Gifford to Murray, postmarked October 20, 1814: "Rowarth has all the Articles except a little thing . . . on Kett, from whom I could not keep my fingers. I had something sent me—but I have changed the tone & made it a high-panegyrick."

308. Article 11. Byron's **Corsair and Lara**

ELLIS, GEORGE. Murray Reg. Murray MS, Gifford to Murray, postmarked Oct 20, 1814: "G E is very eloquent and good." Smiles I, 126. *Gentleman's* XXI, 139. Young 246. *QR* CCX, 747. Graham 41. Clark 238. *CBEL* III, 194

309. Article 12. Leake's Researches in Greece

BLOMFIELD, CHARLES JAMES. Murray Reg. Young 246-47.

310. Article 13. Chalmers's English Poets

SOUTHEY, ROBERT. Murray Reg. Murray MS, Gifford to Murray, postmarked Oct 20, 1814: " We are delayed by Southey, whose continuation I much fear, is gone to Paris after Croker. This Art. I think excellent, I have softened matters a little." Cottle 242-43. Southey 577. Young 246. Spurgeon II, 66: Southey? Graham 41. *CBEL* I, 408. *See also* Warter II, 362

Volume XII, Number 23 (October 1814)
Published by January 14, 1815: Warter II, 395

311. Article 1. Flinder's Voyage to Terra Australis

BARROW, JOHN. Murray Reg. Murray MS, Gifford to Murray [July 26, 1814]: "I wish you could get poor Flinders book for Mr Barrow." Murray MS, Gifford to Murray, postmarked Oct 20, 1814: "Barrow is hard at work on Flinders . . ." Notation on letter: "Flinders, Q. R. 23." *Gentleman's* XXI, 139. *See also* Smiles I, 262

312. Article 2. Wake's Mon Journal de huit Jours; Eustace, Shepherd, Wansey and Planta on Paris

CROKER, JOHN WILSON. Murray Reg. Cites unspecified old letters. Murray MS, Gifford to Murray [1814]: "Has Mr Croker seen the other little publication *Mon voyage de huit Jours?* It is more comical than Wanseys." Brightfield 454

313. Article 3. Chalmers's English Poets

SOUTHEY, ROBERT. Murray Reg. British Museum MS, Southey to Peachey, Feb 1, 1815: "I have been vexed to see that what I had said of your friend Bowles in the last Quarterly has been cut down, & converted by this mutilation into an equivocal kind of complement,—or at best but a cold half-praise,—which I should be the last man to offer. My words were —Bowles—who yet lives to enjoy his fame, & to whom we gladly take the opportunity of returning our thanks for the pleasure & benefit which we derived from his poems in our youth." Cottle 242-43. Southey 577, and 313: "deplorably injured by mutilation." Warter II, 393-94, 395. Greever 120-21: mutilated. Graham 41. Spurgeon II, 66: Southey? Clark 179

314. Article 4. Wells on Dew

YOUNG, THOMAS. Murray Reg. Murray MS, Gifford to Murray, [Nov 18 or 21, 1814]: "I enclose a bit for Rowarth [the printer] from Dr. Y." Brande XXVIII, 157. *Gentleman's* XXI, 139. Pettigrew IV, 21

315. Article 5. Wordsworth's Excursion

LAMB, CHARLES, and GIFFORD, WILLIAM. Murray Reg. Lamb I, 160-72, 446 note. Lucas II, 139 and note, 149-50 and notes. Hutchinson I, 203-16 and note. Selincourt II, 620, 642, 715-16. Knight II, 44. Morley I, 81 and note. Bowles 71. Warter II, 393-94. *Gentleman's* XXI, 140. *CHEL* XII, 213. Graham 41. Holloway in *RES* X, 63. *CBEL* III, 172. *See also* Clark 187, 273 note; Lucas II, 136-39, 146-48 and note, 148; Wordsworth 59; Robinson I, 153
LAMB, CHARLES. Graham in *SP* XXII, 509. Clark 179, 201, 223

316. Article 6. A W Schlegel's Dramatic Literature

HARE-NAYLOR, FRANCIS. Murray Reg.: "F. Hare Naylor or Coleridge." Addit. note: "from a letter of F H N's July 21st 1814 [and] from a letter of S T C's Sept 10, 1814. See also W G July 26/14." Murray MS, Gifford to Murray [July 26, 1814]: "I have got Mrs Hoppner rummaging for Schlegel & Bermingham [?] . . . I think Mr Naylor will do the first well and I shall be very glad to try Mr Hare with the latter." *See also* Griggs II, 126. Apparently Coleridge had no connection.

317. Article 7. Condition of the Poor

? SOUTHEY, ROBERT. Murray Reg.: "Southey." *Gentleman's* XXI, 139. *QR* CCX, 746. But *see* Southey 313, quoted below under Entry 319.

318. Article 8. Thomas Brown's Paradise of Coquettes

COHEN, FRANCIS. Murray Reg. Smiles I, 284-85 and note

319. Article 9. Forbes's Oriental Memoirs

SOUTHEY, ROBERT. Murray Reg. Warter II, 395. Southey 577 and
313: "You would see in the last number [of QR] two articles of mine—
the one upon the History of English Poetry [Entry 313], the other upon
Forbes Travels [Entry 319], both deplorably injured by mutilation." Graham 41

320. Article 10. Layman on Trees, Timber Dry Rot, etc.

BARROW, JOHN. Murray Reg. Addit. note: "from a letter of Barrows
Nov 27, 1814." Smiles I, 284

321. Article 11. Memoirs of Buonaparte's Deposition

CROKER, JOHN WILSON. Murray Reg. Murray MS. Gifford to Murray
[June 3, 1814]: "Mr Croker, who is really a treasure to us, has sent to
say that if we can find a peg, he will give us something on the voyage etc of
Buonaparte to Elba—Nothing can be more desirable. Pray look & see,
if there be among the new publications any trumpery pamphlet (no matter
what) that notices the departure of the cidevant Emperor & King. I really
feel most obliged to my Admiralty friend." Murray MS, Gifford to Murray [July 26, 1814]: "Mr Croker never writes to me so that I know not
whether he will give us Elba. I hope, however, that he will." *Gentleman's*
XXI, 140: Croker? Brightfield 454

Volume XII, Number 24 (January 1815)
Published after February 16: Southey 313

322. Article 1. Stewart's Philosophy of the Human Mind

LYALL, WILLIAM ROWE. Murray Reg. Murray MS, Gifford to Murray
[Jan 27, 1815]: "I will beg you to get a frank for Mr Lyall. His Art...
is truly excellent—but you must never venture into Scotland again without
a coat of mail and a blunderbuss." Smiles I, 284 and note. *DNB. See
also* Dudley 3

323. Article 2. Lewis and Clarke's American Travels

SOUTHEY, ROBERT. Cottle 242-43. Southey 577. Allibone I, 1093. Cairns
I, 46: "credited to Southey." *See also* Warter II, 362, 394, 399; Southey
313
BARROW, JOHN. Murray Reg.

324. Article 3. Gibbon's Miscellaneous Works

WHITAKER, THOMAS DUNHAM. Murray Reg. Nichols xxii and xxix.
Gentleman's XXI, 140. Graham 41

325. Article 4. Louis Buonaparte's Marie

CROKER, JOHN WILSON. Murray Reg. Brightfield 454

326. Article 5. Colquhoun on the British Empire

? SOUTHEY, ROBERT. Murray Reg.: "R. Southey." Murray MS. Gifford to Murray [Nov. 14, 1814]: "I have just rec'd the enclosed from
Southey. It is interesting that he should have taken up Colquhoun—I
have however, told him that his need not prevent his proceeding with the
subject, as he may easily find another book to put at the head of his Art."

327. Article 6. Cunningham's Velvet Cushion

Author not identified. But *see* Entry 316, reading *Cunningham* for *Bermingham.*

328. Article 7. Seppings's Improvements in Ship-building

BARROW, JOHN. Murray Reg. Murray MS, Gifford to Murray [Jany 27, 1815]: "I have put up for Rowarth the 16 first pages of Barrow . . . Mr B's I have desired to be put into pages. . . . I have also sent Mr Barrow's proof which I wish you to convey to him . . ."

329. Article 8. Buonaparte's Russian Campaign

? HAY, ROBERT WILLIAM. Murray Reg.: "R H Hay." A question mark after the name has been crossed out. Addit. note: "? R H Hay from his letter." Then follows a confused Addit. note: "(8 or 9) G Ellis see letter of Mrs. Ellis Dec 23, 1814. See Hays Feb & May 1815." Murray MS, Gifford to Murray [July 26, 1814]: "Mr Hay has written for some book, but I know not what to recommend." Murray MS, Gifford to Murray [Jany 27, 1815]: "I have put up for Rowarth . . . the ms of Mr Hay to be set up as he desired."

330. Article 9. Guy Mannering

CROKER, JOHN WILSON. Murray Reg.: ~~"W Gifford."~~ Addit. note: "in Crokers list this is given as one of his." Another Addit. note cites Murray's marked QR to confirm Croker's authorship. Still another Addit. note may suggest Ellis: "(8 or 9) G Ellis see letter of Mrs Ellis Dec 23, 1814." QR CCX, 741 and note, 775 note. Graham 41. Brightfield 454. Hillhouse 47. See also Jennings I, 84
GIFFORD, WILLIAM. Lockhart V, 150. Gentleman's XXI, 140

331. Article 10. Robert's Letters and Papers

SOUTHEY, ROBERT. Murray Reg. Warter II, 414, 420. Cottle 242-43. Southey 577. Gentleman's XXI, 140. D N B on Barré C Roberts. See also Warter II, 362, 394

Volume XIII, Number 25 (April 1815)
Published June 20: Warter II, 419

332. Article 1. Miot's Mémoires de l'Expédition en Egypte

SOUTHEY, ROBERT. Murray Reg. Cottle 242-43. Southey 577. Warter II, 416-17. See also Warter II, 394, 396, 402, 419; Southey 316

333. Article 2. De Guignes's Dictionnaire Chinois

BARROW, JOHN. Murray Reg. Cites unspecified old letters

334. Article 3. Mason's Account of Ireland

CROKER, JOHN WILSON. Murray Reg. Cites unspecified old letters. Brightfield 454

335. Article 4. Southey's Roderick

BEDFORD, GROSVENOR CHARLES. Murray Reg. Cites Murray's marked QR. Murray MS, Gifford to Murray [1814]: "Grosvenor Bedford was not selected by me . . .—He was fixed upon by Southey himself." Murray MS, Gifford to Murray [Jany 28, 1815]: ". . . the difficulty with me is Southey. He entertains a very high opinion of his friend's talents, as he shewed by employing him & he has seen & approved the critique. . . . he is after all the sheet anchor of the Revw & should not be lightly hurt. Grosvenor Bedford's influence with him is . . . great . . . some little good may be done by a few omissions towards the conclusion . . . you have not the last revise, in which I made a few alterations . . ." Graham 41

336. Article 5. New Covering to Velvet Cushion
Author not identified

337. Article 6. Park's Mission to Africa
BARROW, JOHN. Seymour 28
SOUTHEY, ROBERT. Murray Reg.: "R Southey."

338. Article 7. Elton's Classic Poets
HALLAM, HENRY. Murray Reg. *See also* Smiles I, 285

339. Article 8. Gall and Spurzheim's Physiognomy
Author not identified

340. Article 9. Rice on Irish Grand Jury Laws
CROKER, JOHN WILSON. Murray Reg. Cites unspecified old letters.
Brightfield 454

341. Article 10. Routh's Reliquiae Sacrae
Author not identified

342. Article 11. Wraxall's Historical Memoirs
CROKER, JOHN WILSON. Murray Reg. Brewer MS, Murray to [Crok-
er], n.d.: Urging Croker to fulfill his promise and finish an article on
Wraxall's tales, Murray makes the following suggestions and comments.
Choose extracts such as Sir W. Hamilton's account of Ferdinand. Give
the last part of the pretender, which will permit of much fervor in its con-
temnation. This article should occupy 24 pages [actually 23]. When it is
finished, this issue of Q R will be ready to publish. *Gentleman's* XXI, 140.
Brightfield 454

343. Article 12. Elliott's Life of Wellington
SOUTHEY, ROBERT. Murray Reg. Warter II, 411. Grierson IV, 75 and
note. Cottle 242-43. Southey 577. Smiles I, 270. *Gentleman's* XXI, 140.
QR CCX, 760 note. *See also* Warter II, 399, 402, 419; Ticknor I, 50

Volume XIII, Number 26 (July 1815)
Published between Nov. 2 and Dec. 6: Brewer MS, Murray to Croker, and
Robinson I, 178

344. Article 1. Scott's Lord of the Isles
ELLIS, GEORGE. Murray Reg. Cites Murray's marked QR. Murray MS,
Gifford to Murray, Sept 29, 1815: "I have spoken of Scott in the missing
letter . . . Since that, I have carefully looked over the revise, which I had
previously modified." Smiles I, 126. Graham 41

345. Article 2. Missionary Travels in South Africa
BARROW, JOHN. Murray MS, Gifford to Murray, Sept 6, 1815: "Send
also to Mr. Barrow the second sheet of this No which contains the opening
of his African art." *See also* Young 251.
SOUTHEY, ROBERT. Murray Reg. *See also* Southey 262, 269

346. Article 3. Marsh's Horae Pelasgicae
BLOMFIELD, CHARLES JAMES. Murray Reg.: "~~Ugo Foscolo.~~" Addit.
note: "Bp. Blomfield of London." Cites Murray's marked QR. Another
Addit. note: "See also Blomfield's letter July 2/15."
FOSCOLO, UGO. *Gentleman's* XXI, 140

347. Article 4. Porter's Cruize in the Pacific

BARROW, JOHN. Murray Reg.: "? Barrow" in pencil. Warter III, 11-12:
". . . Barrow . . . persists in discrediting cannibalism. . . ." Cf. *QR* XIII,
367. *See also* Young 251

348. Article 5. Dunlop's History of Fiction

COHEN, FRANCIS (PALGRAVE), and GIFFORD, WILLIAM. Murray Reg.: "F Palgrave (Cohen)." Murray MS, Gifford to Murray, Sept
29, 1815: "Cohen's Art will be very amusing. I have taken much pains
with it . . ." Graham 41 (Palgrave)
TAYLOR, GEORGE. Surtees xiv
? SCOTT, WALTER. Grierson IV, 544 and note

349. Article 6. Translations from the Chinese

? BARROW, JOHN. Murray Reg.: "? Barrow" in pencil

350. Article 7. Gentz on the Fall of Prussia

HAY, ROBERT WILLIAM. Murray Reg. "R W Hay." Addit. note: "from
a letter of R W H's Dec 8, 1816." Brewer MS, Murray to Croker, Nov 2,
1815: "We are waiting for a proof to be sent back from Mr Hay." *See also*
Young 251

351. Article 8. Pillet's L'Angleterre, vue à Londres

CROKER, JOHN WILSON. Murray Reg. Cites unspecified old letters.
Brightfield 454

352. Article 9. Life of Wellington

SOUTHEY, ROBERT. Murray Reg. Murray MS, Gifford to Murray, Sept
29, 1815: "Of Southey's I think very highly, I carried it to our friend
[Croker?] that he might insert the letters etc, as he desired." Brewer Ms,
Murray to Croker, Nov 2, 1815: "Mr Gifford received yesterday the Revise which is not yet worked off & we might yet be in time for the interesting account of the Battle which you mention should you think it
right to trust it to Gifford and Southey who is here on his return from
Brussels . . ." Murray MS, Gifford to Murray, [1815?]: "Mr Southey has
brought back the name of Alexander Davidson . . . for *Alexander Davidson* read an *individual* or *a gentleman* & omit *free spirit* before liberal,
and it may do, though, I do not see the necessity of it." Cf. *QR* XIII,
523. Murray MS, Gifford to Murray, [Nov 25, 1815]: "I wish Southey
had not been quite so obstinate, but his Article is of such surpassing merit
that tis not possible to be long angry. Still our friend [Croker?] has
done it much good unperceived by S." Robinson I, 178. Warter III, 5-6,
13. Cottle 242-43. *Gentleman's* XXI, 140. Young 251. Brightfield 322
Halloway in *RES* X, 63. *See also* Warter II, 411, 413, 416-17, 418, 421-22,
425, 429-30; III, 4; Coleridge 267-68; Southey 317

Volume XIV, Number 27 (October 1815)
Published March 1816: Murray Reg.

353. Article 1. Perceval and Cordiner On Celon

BARROW, JOHN. Murray Reg.

354. Article 2. Bishop of London—Mr. Belsham

D'OYLY, GEORGE. Murray Reg. Murray MS, Gifford to Murray, [Sept 6,
1815]: ". . . I send . . . something from D'Oyly on Belsham . . ."

355. Article 3. Buonaparte [8 pamphlets, one by Miss Williams]

CROKER, JOHN WILSON. Murray Reg. Brewer MS, Murray to [Croker], n.d.: "Will you like to do any more with the article on Buonaparte previous to my setting it up in the regular pages and sheets of the Rev. Do you think you will make any more use of Miss Williams in it, *for instance*. I will at any rate put both copies of your proof in my packet on Monday." *Gentleman's* XXI, 140. Jennings I, 52. Brightfield 454

356. Article 4. Jamieson and Townsend on Ancient Languages

YOUNG, THOMAS. Murray Reg. Brande XXVIII, 157. *Gentleman's* XXI, 140. Pettigrew IV, 21. Young 241. *See also* Young 251

357. Article 5. Lord Blayney's Journey through Spain

CROKER, JOHN WILSON. Murray Reg. Brightfield 454

358. Article 6. Mendicity

BARROW, JOHN. Murray Reg.
SOUTHEY, ROBERT. *Gentleman's* XXI, 140. *See also* Southey 309

359. Article 7. Beatson's Tracts on St. Helena

CROKER, JOHN WILSON. Murray Reg. Brightfield 454

360. Article 8. Elphinstone's Caubul

BARROW, JOHN, and GIFFORD, WILLIAM. Murray Reg. Murray MS, Gifford to Murray, [Feb 24, 1816]: "I was not aware that the first part of Cabul was printed off . . . I should . . . have softened it a little more . . . I have really had a good deal to do with this Art. . . . our Friend has been rather careless in his style." *See also* Smiles I, 287

361. Article 9. Jane Austen's Emma: A Novel

SCOTT, WALTER. Murray Reg. Lockhart VI, 187 note. *Gentleman's* XXI, 140. Douglas I, 336. Smiles I, 289 note. Grierson IV, 167 and note. *QR* CCX, 740-41 and note. Bonnell 370-71 and note. *CHEL* XII, 166. Graham 41-42. Graham in *PMLA* XLIV, 309. Hogan in *PMLA* XLV, 1264-65. Ball 162-64. Keynes 245. Paston 10. Clark 231. *CBEL* III, 383, *See also* Smiles I, 287-90; Grierson IV, 168; Whately iii-iv, and 282 and note; Reitzel in *PMLA* XLIV, 310
WHATELY, RICHARD. Reitzel in *PMLA* XLIII, 492-93. Levy 81-82 and note

362. Article 10. Wordsworth's White Doe

LYALL, WILLIAM ROWE. Murray Reg. Graham 41. *See also* Smiles I, 284; Pfeiffer in *PQ* XI, 107, note 44
WHITAKER, THOMAS DUNHAM. Nichols xxix
GIFFORD, WILLIAM. *Gentleman's* XXI, 140

363. Article 11. Tweddell's Remains

BLOMFIELD, CHARLES JAMES. Murray Reg. Murray MS, Gifford to Murray, [Sept 6, 1815]: "Pray forward the enclosed to Mr Blomfield . . ." Murray MS, Gifford to Murray, [Feb 13, 1816]: "I have put up Twedell for Rowarth [the printer]. I rec'd it this inst from Mr Blomfield with the enclosed letter. . . . I want Elgin having promised Blomfield, as is but just, that he should see it & decide on the appearance of his own art." Murray MS, Gifford to Murray, [February 24, 1816]: "I am glad that Twedell is gone . . . there is very little to be altered." Brewer MS, Murray to [Croker], Sunday [Feb 1816]: see Entry 365. Brewer MS, Murray to [Croker], Sunday Night, [n.d.]: see Entry 365

364. Article 12. Lives of Melancthon and Jeremy Taylor

WHITAKER, THOMAS DUNHAM. Murray Reg. Murray MS, Gifford to Murray, [Feb 13, 1816] : ". . . I mark the remd'r of Dr Whitaker's Art to send him . . . Melanchthon, I have not rec'd from the Dr though I sent it off at once." Nichols xxix

365. Article 13. Elgin on Tweddell's Remains

CROKER, JOHN WILSON. Murray Reg. Brewer MS, Murray to [Croker], Sunday [Feb 1816] : "You have been so bothered with the variety of unexpected documents & obtrusive remarks upon the Elgin Subject that I am almost afraid of forcing any thing more upon your attention—as however what I now send will be the last—I hope your patience will endure it. [¶] Mr G[ifford] sent Mr B[lomfield] a copy of the last proof & it is inclosed with his remarks on and upon it—he is a truly confidential man—with a sound logical head—though he has certainly drawn *all* his prejudices from information collected in the enemy's camp." Brewer MS, Murray to [Croker], Sunday night, n.d.: "I entreat you not to view this matter in the way you do—Mr Blomfield is a particular friend of Mr Gifford & a perfectly confidential Man—but on either side the articles are only shown in confidence to each & his although written three months ago at least is only this moment put in proof—& your article was shewn to him only because he had agreed to cut out from his so long ago sent in the very favourable view wh he had written upon the controversy—these things are done often secretly & no harm comes of them. . . ." Brightfield 454

Volume XIV, Number 28 (January 1816)
Published in May: Murray Reg.

366. Article 1. Culloden Papers

SCOTT, WALTER. Murray Reg. Smiles I, 290. Grierson IV, 167 and note. *Gentleman's* XXI, 140. Scott. Douglas I, 356. *See also* Smiles I, 287, 289-90; Grierson IV, 168; X, 198 and note

367. Article 2. Alfieri's Life and Writings; translated by Charles Lloyd

SOUTHEY, ROBERT. Murray Reg. Cottle 242-43. Southey 577. *CBEL* III, 238. See also Warter II, 394; III, 14-15

368. Article 3. De Humboldt's Travels

BARROW, JOHN. Murray Reg. *Gentleman's* XXI, 140

369. Article 4. Polwhele's Fair Isabel of Cotchele

? SCOTT, WALTER. Murray Reg.: "? Sir W Scott." Addit. note: "See a letter from Sir W S to J M (undated)." Smiles I, 290. Graham 41. *See also* Grierson II, 81-82, 397, 422-23; Smiles I, 290-91

370. Article 5. Beckmann's History of Inventions

BARROW, JOHN. Murray Reg.

371. Article 6. Alison's Sermons

LYALL, WILLIAM ROWE. Murray Reg.

372. Article 7. Hobhouse's Letters from Paris

CROKER, JOHN WILSON. Murray Reg. Brewer MS, Murray to [Croker], n.d.: Murray, urging Croker to write a severe article against Beloe, says: Let it be like Hobhouse, a thing to remain in all times and to be quoted. Broughton I, 342 and note. Brightfield 454. Clark 198: "almost certainly Croker's with perhaps some embellishments by Gifford. . ."

373. Article 8. Tombuctoo—Narrative of Robert Adams

BARROW, JOHN. Murray Reg.

374. Article 9. Leigh Hunt's Rimini

CROKER, JOHN WILSON. Murray Reg. Graham 41. Clark 197-98, 212-13. Brightfield 454
GIFFORD, WILLIAM. Hazlitt 406. *See also* Smiles I, 263 note; Moore VIII, 215

375. Article 10. De Pradt's Congrès de Vienne

HAY, ROBERT WILLIAM. Murray Reg.

376. Article 11. Lord Barrington's Political Life

PHILLPOTTS, HENRY. Murray Reg.

377. Article 12. Elgin Marbles

CROKER, JOHN WILSON. Murray Reg. *Gentleman's* XXI, 140. Jennings I, 84. Brightfield 454. *See also QR* CCX, 753-54

Volume XV, Number 29 (April 1816)
Published in August: Murray Reg.

378. Article 1. La Roche Jacquelein—La Vendée

SOUTHEY, ROBERT. Murray Reg. British Museum MS, Southey to Peachey, Dec 6, 1816: "You may trace me in the Quarterly upon La Vendee & the State of the Poor,—Ali Bey's Travels, & the Foreign Travellers in England." Robinson I, 192. Cottle 242-43. Southey 577. *See also* Southey 329, 330, 331; Warter III, 32

379. Article 2. Milman's Fazio

COLERIDGE, JOHN TAYLOR. Murray Reg. Addit. note: "This was the 3rd Review of Fazio offered to the Editor (*W. G.*)" Murray MS, Gifford to Murray, [Feb 13, 1816]: "I have rec'd another review of Fazio. This is the third, & by far the best. It is in the hand of the young Mr Coleridge and will do extremely well." Graham 41

380. Article 3. Pottinger's Travels in Beloochistan and Sinde

BARROW, JOHN. Murray Reg.

381. Article 4. Monk's Alcestis

BLOMFIELD, CHARLES JAMES. Murray Reg. *CHEL* XII, 526

382. Article 5. Scott's Antiquary

CROKER, JOHN WILSON. Murray Reg. Addit. note: "Not mentioned in Mr Crokers own list." Jennings I, 84. Graham 41. Brightfield 454. Hillhouse 47. *See also* Pfeiffer in PQ XI, 103
GIFFORD, WILLIAM. Lockhart V, 150. *Gentleman's* XXI, 140

383. Article 6. Barbary States

BARROW, JOHN. Murray Reg.

384. Article 7. Lord Blayney's Sequel to his Travels

CROKER, JOHN WILSON. Murray Reg. Brightfield 454

385. Article 8. Reports on the Poor

SOUTHEY, ROBERT. Murray Reg. British Museum MS, Southey to Peachey, Dec. 6, 1816: See Entry 378. Southey 336, 577. Robinson I, 192. Warter III, 47. Williams in Blackwood's CXLIV, 182. Cottle 242-43. *Gentleman's* XXI, 140. Southey *Essays* I, 159. *QR* CCX, 746. Haller in *PMLA* XXXVII, 284-85. *See also* Warter III, 32

386. Article 9. Malcolm's History of Persia

HEBER, REGINALD. Murray Reg. Heber I, 418 and note. *Gentleman's* XXI, 140

Volume XV, Number 30 (July 1816)
Published in November: Murray Reg.

387. Article 1. Travels of Ali Bey

SOUTHEY, ROBERT. Murray Reg. Brewer MS, Murray to Croker, Aug. 18, 1816: ". . . we have already four articles printed—one I have this day been favoured with from Mr B[arrow] [cf. Entry 389 and Entry 394] others from Southey [cf. Entry 398] & Scott [cf. Entry 407] & expect to be able to publish on the first of October . . ." British Museum MS, Southey to Peachey, Dec 6, 1816: "You may trace me in the Quarterly upon La Vendee & the State of the Poor,—Ali Bey's Travels, & the Foreign Travellers in England." Cottle 242-43. Southey 577. *See also* Warter III, 21

388. Article 2. Wedderburne Webster's Waterloo

CROKER, JOHN WILSON. Murray Reg. Smiles I, 371 note. Graham 41. Clark 197-98. Brightfield 454

389. Article 3. Missionary Chinese Works

BARROW, JOHN. Murray Reg. Brewer MS, Murray to Croker, Aug 18, 1816: See Entry 387. *See also* Young 272 note

390. Article 4. Works of Mason

WHITAKER, THOMAS DUNHAM. Murray Reg. Murray MS, Gifford to Murray [Feb 13, 1816]: "He [Whitaker] wishes to do something with Mason, & he will do it well no doubt." Murray MS, Gifford to Murray, [Feb 24, 1816]: "Whitaker . . . had promised to take Mason with which he seemed pleased." Nichols xxix. Graham 41

391. Article 5. Insanity and Madhouses

UWINS, DAVID. Murray Reg.: "Dr Ewens." *Gentleman's* XXI, 140. *DNB*

392. Article 6. Rundall's Symbolic Illustrations

CROKER, JOHN WILSON. Murray Reg. Addit. note: "Not mentioned in Mr Croker's own list." Brightfield 454

393. Article 7. Chateaubriand's Monarchy

CROKER, JOHN WILSON. Murray Reg. Murray MS, Gifford to Murray, [1816]: ". . . as our indefatigable friend [context suggests Croker] is so alert, perhaps he may have Chateaubriand ready . . ." Brightfield 454

394. Article 8. Humboldt's American Researches

BARROW, JOHN. Murray Reg. Murray MS, Gifford to Murray, [Oct. 1816]: ". . . Barrow has this moment sent me back two sheets of Humboldt which I will with all possible speed prepare for Rowarth." Brewer MS, Murray to Croker, Aug 18, 1816: see Entry 387. *See also* Southey 308

395. Article 9. Hogg's Poetic Mirror

CROKER, JOHN WILSON. Murray Reg. Brightfield 454. *See also* Grierson IV, 544 and note

396. Article 10. Baptismal Regeneration—Mant, John Scott, Biddulph etc.

DAVISON, JOHN. Murray Reg.: "R. Davidson." Brewer MS, Murray to [Croker], n.d.: "The Baptismal Article was written by a very eminent Man Mr Davison of Oriel." Davison. *Gentleman's* XXI, 140. *D N B*

397. Article 11. James's Sweden, Prussia etc.

HAY, ROBERT WILLIAM. Murray Reg. Murray MS, Gifford to Murray, [Oct 1816]: ". . . I wished to show [you] the extraordinary letter which I have rec'd from Mr Hay—It has nettled me a little . . ."

398. Article 12. Works on England—Travellers

SOUTHEY, ROBERT. Murray Reg. Brewer MS, Murray to Croker, Aug 18, 1816: see Entry 387. British Museum MS, Southey to Peachey, Dec 6, 1816: see Entry 387. Cottle 243-43. Southey 577. Southey *Essays* I, 251. *Gentleman's* XXI, 140. *See also* Williams in *Blackwood's* CLXIV, 182; Warter III, 44 (on danger of licentious press. Cf. *QR* No. 30, p. 564); Warter III, 47, and 177 (on dangers of publishing details about suicide. Cf. *QR* No. 30 p. 541)

Volume XVI, Number 31 (October 1816)
Published on February 11, 1817: Grierson IV, 363 note

399. Article 1. Legh's Journey in Egypt and Nubia

BARROW, JOHN. Murray Reg.

400. Article 2. Charles Phillips's Poems and Speeches

CROKER, JOHN WILSON. Murray Reg. Brightfield 454

401. Article 3. Sumner's Prize Essay on the Creation

D'OYLY, GEORGE. Murray Reg.
? WEYLAND, JOHN. Ricardo-Trower 47: "Report says that Mr Weyland was the reviewer."

402. Article 4. Campbell's Shipwreck and Adventures

BARROW, JOHN. Murray Reg.

403. Article 5. Becket's Shakespeare's Himself Again

GIFFORD, WILLIAM. Murray Reg.

404. Article 6. Tracts on Saving Banks

? WALKER, WILLIAM SIDNEY. Murray Reg.: "Rev—Walker (Cambridge)"
? LUNDIE, ROBERT. Murray MS, Rt. Lundie, Kelso, to Murray, July 15, 1816: Lundie is sending Murray an article on Savings Banks, which he hopes will be printed in next QR. He thinks the article contains a great deal of curious and little-known information. It was prepared at considerable expense of time and money. Gifford has not told him where to send it. Notation on letter suggests: *QR,* no. 31, Art 6

405. Article 7. Cowper's Poems and Life

WALKER, WILLIAM SIDNEY. Murray Reg.: "Rev—Walker (Cambridge)"

406. Article 8. Lord Selkirk and the North-West Company

BARROW, JOHN. Murray Reg. *Gentleman's* XXI, 140

407. Article 9. Byron's Childe Harold III, and other Poems

SCOTT, WALTER. Murray Reg. Brewer MS, Murray to Croker, Aug 18, 1816: ". . . we have already four articles printed—one I have this day been favoured with from Mr B others from Southey & Scott . . ." Grierson IV, 296 and note; IV, 363 and note; VII, 116 note. Byron II, 41. Seymour 173. Russell I, 191. Douglas I, 356, 379 note, 413 and note, 422 note. *Gentleman's* XXI, 140. Ball 162-64. Graham 41. *CBEL* III, 192, 196. *See also* Smiles I, 374-75; Douglas I, 371 note; Grierson IV, 149 (cf. *QR* XVI, 191-96, on Waterloo, Napoleon, and Byron); IV, 409; XII, 426 and note; Jennings I, 87; Lambert in *HLQ* II, 341

408. Article 10. Warden's Conversations with Buonaparte

CROKER, JOHN WILSON. Murray Reg. *Gentleman's* XXI, 140. Brightfield 454

409. Article 11. Parliamentary Reform

SOUTHEY, ROBERT. Murray Reg. Cottle 242-43. Southey 577 and 350: "emasculated." Southey *Essays* I, 327. Smiles I, 306 note; II, 40-41. Warter III, 62. *Gentleman's* XXI, 140. Graham 12. *See also* Southey 345; Warter III, 51-52, 56-57, 69

Volume XVI, Number 32 (January 1817)
Published in April 1817: Murray Reg.

410. Article 1. Riley's Shipwreck and Captivity

? SOUTHEY, ROBERT. Murray Reg.: "R. Southey." *See also* Smiles II, 40; Lockhart V, 33

411. Article 2. Ambrosian Manuscripts

BLOMFIELD, CHARLES JAMES. Murray Reg.

412. Article 3. Miss Plumptre's Residence in Ireland

CROKER, JOHN WILSON. Murray Reg. Cites unspecified old letters. Smiles II, 44. Clark 178 and 197-98. Brightfield 454

413. Article 4. Koster's Travels in Brazil

SOUTHEY, ROBERT. Murray Reg. Cottle 242-43. Southey 577. Warter III, 484 (mutilated), and IV, 520 (mutilated). *See also* Warter III, 17 and 48; Smiles II, 40

414. Article 5. Miss Porden's Veils; a Poem

Author not identified

415. Article 6. Lord Amherst's Embassy—Chinese Drama

Author not identified

416. Article 7. Repton on Landscape Gardening

Author not identified

417. Article 8. Scott's Tales of My Landlord

SCOTT, WALTER; and GIFFORD, WILLIAM; and ERSKINE, WIL-
LIAM. Graham 41: "Scott (Gifford and Erskine?)." Graham in *MLN*
XLI, 45. Clark 187-89 and 273 note 98
SCOTT, WALTER, and GIFFORD, WILLIAM. *QR* CCX, 741-44 and note
SCOTT, WALTER, and ERSKINE, WILLIAM. Lockhart IV, 313-14 and
note. Scott XIX, Art. XIII and note. Fyfe 246. *TLS* 1918, 530. Ball
162-64. Canongate I, xix. Grierson IV, 388-89 and note. Lang in *Sketch*
VIII, Supplement, p. 2. *See also* Smiles I, 375-76; Grierson IV, 365 and
note; IV, 379 and note; Grierson's *Scott* 161; Lockhart IV, 311-12; *D N B*
on Erskine
SCOTT, WALTER. Murray Reg.: "Sir W. Scott." Lockhart IV, 313.
Gentleman's XXI, 140. Douglas I, 398. Paston 11-12. Grierson IV, 386
note. Grierson's *Scott* 137. Hillhouse 17 and note, and 50. *See also* Smiles
I, 471; Grierson IV, 544 and note; VII, 360; Sharpe II, 190-91
SENIOR, NASSAU WILLIAM. Levy 81-82 and notes. But *see* Senior,
which omits this essay

418. Article 9. Buonaparte's Appeal to the British Nation

CROKER, JOHN WILSON. Murray Reg. *Gentleman's* XXI, 140. Brightfield 454
SOUTHEY, ROBERT. Seymour 173

419. Article 10. Rise and Progress of Popular Disaffection

SOUTHEY, ROBERT. Murray Reg. Cottle 242-43. Southey 360-61 and
note, 577. Southey *Essays* II, 35. *Gentleman's* XXI, 140. Seymour 173.
White 363, 393. *See also* Southey 350; Warter III, 62 and 69; Smiles II,
40

Volume XVII, Number 33 (April 1817)
Published in August: Murray Reg.

420. Article 1. Burney and Mariner's Accounts of the Tonga Islands

SOUTHEY, ROBERT. Murray Reg. Cottle 242-43. Southey 577. *See also*
Warter III, 61-62; Southey 350

421. Article 2. Dugald Stewart's Dissertation on Philosophy

LYALL, WILLIAM ROWE. Murray Reg. Addit. note: "on the authority
of his nephew Canon Pearson."

422. Article 3. Raffle's History of Java

Author not identified

423. Article 4. Miss Edgeworth's Comic Dramas

Author not identified

424. Article 5. East India College by the Rev. T. R. Malthus

Author not identified

425. Article 6. Hazlitt's Round Table

? RUSSELL, JAMES. Murray Reg. in pencil: "? A Mr. Russell in memoir"
[i.e. in Smiles's *Memoir of Murray*]. Smiles II, 44. Graham 41. Graham
in *SP* XXII, 506. Clark 213. *See, however,* Entry 487
GIFFORD, WILLIAM. Hazlitt 395-401. *See also* Smiles I, 263 note;
Robinson I, 210

426. Article 7. Clarke's Travels (Vols III and IV)

   ? SOUTHEY, ROBERT. *Gentleman's* XXI, 140: Southey

427. Article 8. Paris in 1815, a Poem

   CROKER, JOHN WILSON. Murray Reg. Cites unspecified old letters. Murray MS, Gifford to Murray, [erroneous notation on outside: 1819-20]: "I have been obliged to alter the conclusion of Paris . . . but it was a repetition . . ." Brewer MS, Murray to Croker, n.d.: "Crawley wrote to thank me for the Number of the Review—adding that the article on Paris was uncommonly flattering." Brightfield 454

428. Article 9. Péron: Voyage de Découvertes (Tome II)

   BARROW, JOHN. Murray Reg. *Gentleman's* XXI, 140

429. Article 10. The Tragic Drama—The Apostate, by Richard Sheil

   MATURIN, CHARLES ROBERT, and GIFFORD, WILLIAM. Murray Reg.: "C. R. Maturin." Addit. note: "from a letter of his dated Oct 3 1817." Murray MS, Gifford to Murray [1817]: "I enclose the Apostate for Rowarth. A more potatoe-headed arrangement I never saw—or rather derangement. I have endeavoured to bring some order out of the choas . . . I have reduced its bulk from 19 to about 14 pages." Notation at top of letter: "Maturin's Review of Shiell's Apostate." Brewer MS, Murray to Croker, n.d.: "The Article on the Apostate is by Mathurin." Scott-Maturin 73 note. Idman 179 and 316 Notes III, 2: Maturin. Graham 41: Maturin. Clark 179. *DNB* on Maturin. *See also* Smiles I, 293; Grierson XII, 361-62; Scott-Maturin 82

430. Article 11. France, by Lady Morgan

   CROKER, JOHN WILSON, and GIFFORD, WILLIAM. Murray Reg.: "J. W. Croker." Cites unspecified old letters. Addit. note in pencil: "? Frere. See his letter here enclosed." Murray MS, J. H. Frere to Murray, [n.d.]: "I wish very much to have Ly Morgan—I have done I think a sheet . . . just in the proper way . . . a rodomantade of humourous nonsense . . . the most *laughable nonsense* that I ever did." Pencil notation on letter: "? Q R 33 Art 11." Murray MS, Gifford to Murray [1816]: "Frere is excellent—his letter shall be taken care of." Brewer MS, Gifford to Murray, postmarked Aug 16, 1817: "There are good hopes for the next No [of QR] but I am anxious to get out this, & therefore would have you quicken Mr Frere, now that he has mentioned his purpose. Do you think that it will be advisable to delay publication beyond the 1st of September? The paper truly will be highly desirable. Try to ascertain this, before you leave town. Represent to him, the necessity of losing no time." Murray MS, Gifford to Murray [erroneous notation on outside: "1819-20." Allusion to article on Paris (see Entry 427) establishes 1817]: "The Art [on Lady Morgan] seems . . . formal & somewhat tending toward a pleading . . . it is shrewd, & convincing, &, I think, powerful . . . Pray let Mr Smith copy out for me from the preface that part in which she notices the advice to her in our former No. I think more may be made of it." Brewer MS, Murray to Croker, n.d.: The Marchioness of Abercorn called to express her gratification at seeing Lady Morgan so justly exposed in the Review. Many others have done the same,—a few of them thinking it too violent, but none thinking it unjust. Jennings I, 102, Croker to Peel, Nov 26, 1817: "I wrote the main part . . . but . . . was called away to Ireland when it was in the press; and I am sorry to say that some blunders crept in accidentally, and one or two were premeditatedly added . . ." Clark 196-99: "does not seem like Croker's work." Suggests Gifford. Pfeiffer in *PQ* XI, 101 and 412, Gifford to Murray, 1817: "I am not surprised at what C says of Lady Morgan . . . The criticism, however, must be softened . . ."

CROKER, JOHN WILSON. Murray Reg. Cites unspecified old letters. For Addit. note, see above, under Croker and Gifford. *Gentleman's* XXI, 140. Jennings I, 98. Brightfield 332 note, 333, and 454. Pfeiffer in *PQ*, XI 105 and 412. *See also* Smiles II, 65; Warter III, 78, 78-79; Fitzpatrick 189-90 and 198

Volume XVII, Number 34 (July 1817)
Published in November: Murray Reg.

431. Article 1. History of Discoveries in Africa, by John Leyden

BARROW, JOHN. Murray Reg. Addit. note: "from a letter of J B's Sept 1, 1817." *See also* Seymour 28; Moore VIII, 231; Lockhart V, 29-31 and 33

432. Article 2. Heber's Bampton Lectures

D'OYLY, GEORGE. D'Oyly 24: George D'Oyly's reviews for *QR* include "one, in the thirty-fifth [actually 34th] number of Heber's Bampton Lectures (on the personality, and office, of the Christian Comforter)."

433. Article 3. History of Hofer and the Tyrol

Author not identified

434. Article 4. Malthus on Population

SUMNER, JOHN BIRD. Murray Reg.: "? Sharon Turner." Addit. note: "See Mr Malthus's letter Dec 1st." Murray MS, T R Malthus to Murray, Dec 1, 1817: "I rather guess from internal evidence that the article is by Mr Sumner." Malthus's *S* could easily be mistaken for a *T*. Ricardo-Trower 46-47 and note

435. Article 5. Himalaya Mountains and Lake Manasawara by Colebrooke and Moorcroft

? BARROW, JOHN. Murray Reg.: "? John Barrow." Addit. note: "See same letter [as cited in Entry 431: i.e. "letter of J B's Sept 1, 1817"]"

436. Article 6. French Theatres

CROKER, JOHN WILSON. Murray Reg. Cites unspecified old letters. Brightfield 454

437. Article 7. Chalmers on the Christian Revelation

WHITAKER, THOMAS DUNHAM. Nichols xxix

438. Article 8. Embassy to China

BARROW, JOHN. Murray Reg. Addit. note: "See John Barrows letter Sept 2/1817"

439. Article 9. Letters from Cape of Good Hope in Reply to Mr Warden

CROKER, JOHN WILSON. Murray Reg. Cites unspecified old letters. *Gentleman's* XXI, 140. Brightfield 454

440. Article 10. Spain and her Colonies

? WELLESLEY, RICHARD COLLEY. Murray Reg.: "? R Wellesley" in pencil. Murray MS, R Wellesley [to John Murray], Aug 28, 1817: The promised contribution, which will soon be finished, will not advocate either party. Murray MS, R Wellesley to Murray, Brighton, Oct 3, 1817: "I have concluded and sent to you the article on South American affairs... I have expressed my real opinions—Mr Gifford is perfectly welcome to make any correction in the style or arrangement . . ." Pencil notation on letter: "? Author of Art 10 in Q R *No.* 34."

Volume XVIII, Number 35 (October 1817)
Published in February 1818: Murray Reg.

441. Article 1. Lord Holland's Lope de Vega

SOUTHEY, ROBERT. Murray Reg. British Museum MS, Southey to Peachey, March 24, 1818: "You may have traced me in the account of Lope de Vega in the last QR." Cottle 242-43. Southey 363 and 577. Warter IV, 259. *Gentleman's* XXI, 140. *See also* Southey 358; Warter III, 78 and 81

442. Article 2. Wilks's Sketch of the South of India
Author not identified

443. Article 3. Lives of Haydn and Mozart
Author not identified

444. Article 4. Southey's History of Brazil (Vol II)

HEBER, REGINALD. Murray Reg. Smiles II, 39. Heber I, 456 and note. *Gentleman's* XXI, 140

445. Article 5. Bentham's Plan of Parliamentary Reform
Author not identified

446. Article 6. Humboldt's Travels (Part II)
BARROW, JOHN. *Gentleman's* XXI, 141

447. Article 7. Sir William Adams on Cataract
Author not identified

448. Article 8. Savigny's Naufrage de la Méduse
Author not identified

449. Article 9. Godwin's Mandeville

CROKER, JOHN WILSON. Murray Reg. Cites unspecified old letters. Brewer MS, Murray to [Croker], n.d.: "I hope you will send me a happy 6 pages on Godwin." Graham 41. Brightfield 454

450. Article 10. Kendall's Appeal of Murder and Trial by Battle
Author not identified

451. Article 11. On the Polar Ice and Northern Passage into the Pacific

BARROW, JOHN. Murray Reg. Murray MS, Gifford to Murray [1818]: "I forgot to ask Mr Barrow about the running title—*Passage into the Pacific*, is not sufficiently explanatory . . ." Barrow 505-6 and note. Smiles II, 45 and note. *Gentleman's* XXI, 141

452. Article 12. Malo's Panorama d'Angleterre

CROKER, JOHN WILSON. Murray Reg. *Gentleman's* XXI, 141. Brightfield 454

453. Article 13. Life of Richard Watson, Bishop of Landaff

WHITAKER, THOMAS DUNHAM. Murray Reg. Murray MS, Gifford to Murray, [August 1818]: ". . . Dr W . . . I regard as the best and most forcible painter of character in this country. His Watson, though it was improperly timed, . . . is yet the most striking Art. that I have seen on the subject . . ." Nichols xxix. *Gentleman's* XXI, 141

Volume XVIII, Number 36 (January 1818)
Published in June 1818: Murray Reg.

454. Article 1. Poor Laws

SOUTHEY, ROBERT. Murray Reg. Smiles II, 48. *Gentleman's* XXI, 140. *QR* CCX, 746. *See also* Warter III, 79
RICKMAN, JOHN. Graham 12-13. Graham in *PQ* II, 106

455. Article 2. Basil Hall's Account of the Loo-choo Islands

Author not identified. Murray Reg.: "Mr Hamilton." Murray MS, Gifford to Murray, [June 1818]: "I wish you would look at the Revise—you can form a better guess than I can whether what I have struck out, will leave room for the insertion of those parts of Mr Hamilton's ms which are no[t] crossed. If not—the note on the Memnon on p. 308 [368] must be struck out . . . The note is certainly creditable to Mr Hamilton's judgment and taste." That MS letter probably was the basis for Murray Reg.'s ascription of Art 2 (pp 308-24) to Hamilton. However, examination of *QR* XVIII shows that "page 308" (Art 2) is a mistake for p. 368 (Art 4): see Entry 457. *See also* Grierson V, 116.

456. Article 3. Leigh Hunt's Foliage

? CROKER, JOHN WILSON. Murray Reg.: "J W Croker." Cites unspecified old letters. Graham 41: Croker. Clark 197-98 and 213-14: Croker. Brightfield 454: Croker. *See also* Jennings I, 134; Smiles II, 322, where Croker in 1831 says of Hunt: ". . . I know neither him nor his works, except 'Rimini' "; White 124-25, 363, and 393
? COLERIDGE, JOHN TAYLOR. White 124-25, 363, and 393: "by J W Croker or J T Coleridge"
SOUTHEY, ROBERT. Smiles I, 399, quotes Byron's letter to Murray, Nov 24, 1818, ascribing the article to Southey

457. Article 4. Congo Expedition—African Discoveries

SALT, HENRY; and BARROW, JOHN; and HAMILTON, WILLIAM RICHARD. Murray Reg.: "—Salt (Consul in Egypt)." Murray MS, Gifford to Murray [June 1818]: "I wish you would look at the Revise— you can form a better guess than I can whether what I have struck out, will leave room for the insertion of those parts of Mr Hamilton's ms which are no[t] crossed. If not—the note on the Memnon on p. 308 [actually on p. 368; i.e., Art 4] must be struck out—and this, I suppose, would grieve Mr Barrow—The note is certainly creditable to Mr Hamilton's judgment and taste." Salt I, 491: Hall believes the article was "compiled from documents sent over by Mr Salt." *Gentleman's* XXI, 414: Documents furnished by Salt.

458. Article 5. Mary Shelley's Frankenstein

CROKER, JOHN WILSON. Murray Reg. Cites unspecified old letters. Brewer MS, Murray to Croker, n.d.: After urging Croker to write a major article on the old regime in Louis XV's France [cf. Entry 490], Murray suggests topics for three minor articles: "Frankenstein, Sir P. Francis, & Beloe—Three hours hammering would convert into Poker, Tongs & Shovel & put into instant use—& if I had these four subjects—my Quart[erly Review] is full." Graham 41. Brightfield 454

459. Article 6. Williams's Origin and State of the Indian Army

MALCOLM, JOHN. Murray Reg. Murray MS, Gifford to Murray, [June 1818]: "Sir John [Malcolm?] may certainly follow Frankenstein." *DNB*. *See also* Smiles II, 29

460. Article 7. Douglas on the Passage of Rivers: Military Bridges

SCOTT, WALTER. Murray Reg.: "Sir W Scott" in pencil. Lockhart V, 86, and IX, 277. *Gentleman's* XXI, 140. Douglas II, 2. *See also* Grierson V, 109, 112, 136; Smiles II, 9, 11, 15; Lockhart V, 100

461. Article 8. Burney on Behring's Strait and the Polar Basin

BARROW, JOHN. Murray Reg. *Gentleman's* XXI, 141

462. Article 9. Hazlitt's Characters of Shakespeare's Plays

? RUSSELL, JAMES. Graham in *SP* XXII, 506: "Russell was probably the reviewer. . ." Clark 213-14: "probably by Russell." *See,* however, Entry 487
GIFFORD, WILLIAM. Hazlitt 417-32. Clark 213-14: ". . . attributed to Gifford, but it does not have many of the earmarks of his work."

463. Article 10. Account of the Pindarries

JERDAN, WILLIAM. Jerdan III, 66. *See also* Brightfield 257
? ELLIS, HENRY. Murray Reg.: "? H Ellis." Addit. note: "See H E's letter undated." Murray MS, Henry Ellis to Murray, Saturday [? March 1818]: "It [i.e., some MS that Ellis had been reading for Murray] contains very little new matter upon the most interesting point, the Pindarries themselves. it would however form a good text for an article in the next Quarterly upon the present state of India and I should have no objection to undertake it." Notation on outside of letter: "See QR 36 Art 10"

464. Article 11. Ancient and Modern Greenland

COHEN, FRANCIS. Murray Reg.: "F Cohen." Addit. note: "from a letter of Mr Giffords." Murray MS, Gifford to Murray [May 18, 1818]: "I send the revise . . . I wish you could induce our friend to make a few additions. The passage respecting Saabye's garden . . . would give a good picture of the horticulture of Greenland of which scarcely anything is said . . . the good priest's journey . . . should be compressed . . . I think Thorgill [see *QR* XVIII, pp. 487-90] long, but I can shorten it no more." Smiles II, 46. Palgrave. Clark 178: revised considerably by Gifford.

465. Article 12. Ecclesiastical Computation of Easter

? BOSWELL, ALEXANDER. Murray MS, Gifford to Murray, [May-June 1818]: "What if between Greenland [i.e., Entry 464] and Pindarries [Entry 463], we place Boswell (if he can be got ready) . . ." Smiles II, 47: probably by Boswell

466. Article 13. Kirkton's History of the Church of Scotland

SCOTT, WALTER. Murray Reg. Lockhart V, 86, 99 note, and IX, 277. Scott. *Gentleman's* XXI, 140. Grierson IV, 379 and note; V, 108-9 and note; V, 135-36 and note. Douglas II, 2. *See also* Smiles II, 9, 11, 15; Grierson IV, 485 and note; IV, 487 and note; IV, 508 and note; V, 35 and 141; Sharpe II, 147, 150, 163

Volume XIX, Number 37 (April 1818)
Published in September 1818: Murray Reg.

467. Article 1. Evelyn's Memoirs

SOUTHEY, ROBERT. Murray Reg. Cites unspecified old letters. Murray MS, Gifford to Murray [August 1818]: ". . . A great card [aid?] was lost when Southey was set upon Evelyn, in preference to Dr W[hitaker]. . . ." Cottle 242-43. Southey 577. Warter III, 100 and 103. Smiles II, 48. *Gentleman's* XXI, 141. Graham 41. *See also* Grierson V, 140; XII, 433-34; Warter III, 93-94, 99; Smiles II, 11, 12, 43.

468. Article 2. Birkbeck's Notes on America

BARROW, JOHN, and GIFFORD, WILLIAM. Murray Reg.: "? Barrow & Gifford" in pencil. Cites unspecified old letters. Addit. note: "I am very glad that you sent Birkbeck, he appears to be the most dangerous man that ever wrote from America . . . our friend (?) had missed his character & I have nearly rewritten the Art. *Wm Gifford!*" Brewer MS, Murray to [Croker], n.d.: "I send Birkbeck's two works." Murray MS, Gifford to Murray, July 19, [1818]: "Rowarth has the whole of Evelyn, & I only wait to know if Barrow means to notice Birkbeck's 2d work, to proceed." Murray MS, Gifford to Murray, postmarked Ramsgate, [August 1818]: "Your Review of Birkbeck [i.e., a review that Murray has forwarded to Gifford at Ramsgate?] is not only what you call it—mischievous—but *malicious,* absurd and dull—evincing no talent whatever." Murray MS, Gifford to Murray, postmarked Ramsgate, August 4, 1818: "I am very glad that you have sent Birkbeck. He appears to me the most dangerous man that ever yet wrote from America, & is likely to do us much mischief. Our friend had missed his character; and I have nearly re-written the Art." Smiles II, 51

469. Article 3. On the Means of Improving the People

SOUTHEY, ROBERT, and RICKMAN, JOHN. Southey 361-62. Warter III, 100. Rickman 10 (by Rickman); 134 (nominally by Southey); 195-204 (largely by Rickman; about two pages by Southey).
SOUTHEY, ROBERT. Murray Reg. Southey 361 and 577. Cottle 242-43. Southey *Essays* II, 111. *Gentleman's* XXI, 141. *QR* CCX, 746. Graham 16. *See also* Warter III, 88 and 99

470. Article 4. Walpole's Letters to Montagu

SCOTT, WALTER. Murray Reg.: "~~J W Croker~~" Cites unspecified old letters. "Sir W. Scott." Cites unspecified old letters. Addit. note: "Not mentioned in Mr Croker's own list." Murray MS, Gifford to Murray, postmarked August 4, 1818: "I wish our friend had put a little of the spirit of his novel stile into his Walpole." Grierson V, 109 and note; V, 130 and note. Graham 41. See also Smiles II, 8, 9, 11, 12; Lockhart V, 100 and 140
CROKER, JOHN WILSON. For details, see under Scott. *Gentleman's* XXI, 141

471. Article 5. Wilson's Military and Political Power of Russia

HEBER, REGINALD. Murray Reg.: "? Reg Heber" in pencil. Cites unspecified old letters. Murray MS, Gifford to Murray, postmarked Aug 4, 1818: ". . . the more I see of Heber's [article], the more I like it. It is really excellent. I have tried to shorten it, but it hangs together so artfully, that I can do very little." Heber I, 458-59 and note. Smiles II, 77-78. *Gentleman's* XXI, 141

472. Article 6. Light's Travels in Egypt, Nubia etc.

SALT, HENRY, and BARROW, JOHN. Murray Reg.: "J Barrow." Murray MS, Barrow to Murray, July 24, 1818: "What shall I do with the papers on Light. There is a drawing . . . of Cephrenes that must occupy a page of the Quarterly, but it consists merely of *lines* [see *QR* XIX, p. 197]. I hope to be ready in 8 or 10 days." Salt I, 491: the article appears "to have been compiled from documents sent over by Mr Salt . . ." *Gentleman's* XXI, 141: ". . . compiled from documents sent over by Mr Salt."

473. Article 7. Keats's Endymion

CROKER, JOHN WILSON. Murray Reg. Cites unspecified old letters. Addit. note: "The original MS in the possession of J M" *QR* CCX, 754-

55. *CHEL* XIII, 266. Graham 21 and 41. Graham in *SP* XXII, 501. Clark 197-98 and 232-33. Paston 31. Brightfield 455. *DNB. See also* Milman 80

GIFFORD, WILLIAM. *DNB:* probably by Gifford. *See also* Clark 232-33

474. Article 8. O'Reilly's Voyage to Davis's Strait

BARROW, JOHN. Murray Reg.

475. Article 9. Byron's Childe Harold, Canto IV

SCOTT, WALTER. Murray Reg. Murray MS, Gifford to Murray, postmarked Ramsgate, [August 1818]: "I like Scott's Childe Harold; it is written with the feeling of a poet." Smiles I, 397 and note; I, 400; II, 13 and note. Grierson V, 223 and note; XII, 433-34 and note. Lockhart V, 173 and note; IX, 278. Scott. *Gentleman's* XXI, 141. Douglas II, 2. Graham 41. *CBEL* III, 192. Corson 280. *See also* Smiles II, 11; Grierson V, 140, 168, 176

476. Article 10. Walpole's Memoirs on Turkey

? BLOMFIELD, CHARLES JAMES. Murray Reg.: "? 10 Bp Blomfield (London)." Murray MS, Gifford to Murray, Ryde, July 19, [1818]: "I shall send Rowarth, in this parcel, Mr Blomfield's ms which does very well." Murray MS, Gifford to Murray, postmarked Ramsgate, August 6, [1818]: Gifford is sending to Murray "A packet which should be franked to Mr Blomfield, whose present residence I do not know—but suppose it to be near Chesterfield."

477. Article 11. Barrett's Woman; a Poem

COLERIDGE, JOHN TAYLOR. Murray Reg.: "Coleridge" in pencil. Cites unspecified old letters. Murray MS, Gifford to Murray, postmarked Ramsgate [August 1818]: "Mr Barrett's parcel contained a sprightly & well-written review of his second Woman.—It is by a friend, who can be useful, if encouraged." Murray MS, Gifford to Murray, Ramsgate, postmarked August 4, 1818: "Coleridge & D'oyly I will send to Rowarth as soon as I have read them carefully over."

478. Article 12. Bellamy's Translation of the Bible

D'OYLY, GEORGE. Murray Reg. Cites unspecified old letters. Addit. note: "See G D O's letter Oct 30/18" Murray MS, Gifford to Murray, Ramsgate, postmarked August 4, 1818: "Coleridge [Entry 477] & D'Oyly I will send to Rowarth as soon as I have read them carefully over." Murray MS, Gifford to Murray, postmarked Ramsgate, August 6, [1818]: Gifford is sending to Murray "D'Oyly for Rowarth. . ." D'Oyly 24. Smiles II, 15 and note

GOODHUGH, WILLIAM. *Gentleman's* XXI, 141. *DNB*

Volume XIX, Number 38 (July 1818)
Published in January 1819: Murray Reg.

479. Article 1. Henderson's Iceland

? BARROW, JOHN. Murray Reg.: "? Barrow." Addit. note: "See letter of J B July 24." Murray MS, Barrow to Murray, July 24, 1818: "If your poetical friend [i.e. Cohen?] means to take up Iceland, I shall lay it down . . . I had actually begun a review of Ebenezer Henderson's tour . . . I think it too serious and too much of a matter-of-fact volume for your flighty friend." Annotation on letter suggests *QR* No. 38, Art 1. Murray Ms, Gifford to Murray, postmarked Ramsgate, August 6, [1818]: "Barrow—Why should he not take Henderson? It would not interfere with Cohen."

480. Article 2. Maturin's Women, a Tale

CROKER, JOHN WILSON. Murray Reg. Cites unspecified old letters. Graham 41. Brightfield 455

481. Article 3. Milman's Samor

COLERIDGE, JOHN TAYLOR. British Museum MS, Southey to Peachey, Feb 9, 1819: "There is nothing of mine in the last Quarterly. The reviewal of Henry Milman's poem is I think the best piece of poetical criticism that has appeared in the Journal. I believe it is written by John Coleridge." Coleridge 277. Milman 38.

482. Article 4. Colden's Life of Fulton—Torpedoes, Steam-boats, etc.

? BARROW, JOHN. Murray MS, Gifford to Murray, postmarked Ramsgate, August 6, [1818]: "Fulton cannot come into this No unless Mr B[arrow?] wishes it, & there is enough of America."

483. Article 5. Moore's History of Small Pox and Vaccination

UWINS, DAVID. Murray MS, Gifford to Murray, postmarked Ramsgate, August 4, 1818: ". . . Uwin's paper . . . is a very good one." *Gentleman's* XXI, 141. *DNB*

484. Article 6. Sir R. Phillips on the Universe

Author not identified

485. Article 7. Brown's Northern Courts

Author not identified

486. Article 8. Davison—Antiquities of Egypt

BARROW, JOHN; YOUNG, THOMAS; and SALT, HENRY. Murray Reg.: "Dr Young? & Barrow." Apparently the article was at first assigned to Young, for the "? & Barrow" is written on a line slightly higher than "Dr Young." Presumably the question mark applies to Barrow's part in the article and not to Young's part. Brande XXVIII, 157, attributes to Young the "Restoration and Translation of the [Greek] Inscription on the Sphynx," on p. 411 of *QR* XIX. Actually the transcription, restoration, and translation occupy two pages: pp. 411-12 of the article. And p. 411 specifically assigns to Young the work of restoring and translating. *Gentleman's* XXI, 141, says the article was compiled from documents sent over by Salt. Young 240-41: Barrow, aided by Young. Pettigrew IV, 21: Young did the restoration and translation of the inscription on the Sphinx. *See also* Salt II, 127

487. Article 9. Hazlitt's English Poets

BARRETT, EATON STANNARD, and GIFFORD, WILLIAM. Murray Reg.: "Mr Russell [and] W Gifford." Cites unspecified old letters. However, as the MS letters from Gifford show [see below], the name "Russell" is a mistaken reading for "Barrett." Murray MS, Gifford to Murray, postmarked Ramsgate, [August 1818]: "Mr Barrett's parcel contained a sprightly & well written review of his second Woman [i.e. Barrett's second poem entitled *Woman*: see Entry 477]—It is by a friend. . . . B himself is at work upon a review of modern poetry for the next No." Murray MS, Gifford to Murray, Ramsgate, postmarked August 4, 1818: "I have a review of Hazlitt by Mr Barrett."
GIFFORD, WILLIAM. Hazlitt 432-41. Spurgeon II, 96
RUSSELL, JAMES. Murray Reg.: "Mr Russell [and] W Gifford." Cites unspecified old letters. However, "Mr Russell" is a misreading for "Mr Barrett": see MS letters quoted above, under Barrett and Gifford. Graham 41. Clark 215

488. Article 10. Sir James Smith's Cambridge Botanical Professorship

   ? D'OYLY, GEORGE. Murray MS, Gifford to Murray, [1818]: "I send you Hodden [or Flodden? or Bellamy?] for Mr D'Oyly, & the volume of Sir James—The latter is the most ignorant & impudent work that the press has lately produced. It must not & shall not escape—tell Mr D'Oyly this."

489. Article 11. Bellamy's Reply to Quarterly Review

   D'OYLY, GEORGE. Murray MS, Gifford to Murray, [1818]: see Entry 488. D'Oyly 24

   GOODHUGH, WILLIAM. Murray Reg.: "—Goodhugh." *Gentleman's* XXI, 141

490. Article 12. Dangeau's Mémoires de Louis XIV

   CROKER, JOHN WILSON. Murray Reg. Cites unspecified old letters. Brewer MS, Murray to [Croker], n.d.: Murray is sending Croker a borrowed copy of Dangeau. Brewer MS, Murray to Croker, n.d.: "The last [?] sheet of Dangeau—is thank God worked off—or we should never be out—& your note may be passed off in another number." Brightfield 455

491. Article 13. Sir Robert Wilson's Letter to the Borough Electors: A Reply

   ? CROKER, JOHN WILSON. Brewer MS, Murray to [Croker], n.d.: "I hope to send you on Monday a new work of Sir Robert Wilson—an account of his own operations in Spain—if you did not appropriate this I think of introducing it to Capt. Pasley." Brewer MS, Murray to Croker, n.d.: "I sent you Sir Robert Wilson's Work which really fills up the Cup & I hope you will make it the occasion, after exposing its falsity & folly, of a severe but dignified exposition & castigation of this set of people—I hope also that you will notice & account for the folly of people generally who appear so eager to be *made unhappy* by such people . . ."

492. Article 14. Mr Brougham—Education Committee

   MONK, JAMES HENRY, and GIFFORD, WILLIAM. Murray Reg.: "Rev Prof Monk (in part)." Addit. note in pencil: "Canning—Croker & Gifford assisting." Murray MS, Gifford to Murray, [January 22, 1819]: ". . . thank God I have been able to complete my design. I have tried to satisfy Monk & brought in any scrap that I could." Notation on letter: QR 38 last article." Monk in *Athenaeum*, No. 2472, pp. 393-95.

   MONK, JAMES HENRY; GIFFORD, WILLIAM; CANNING, GEORGE; and CROKER, JOHN WILSON. Murray Reg.: "Rev Prof Monk (in part)." Addit. note in pencil: "Canning—Croker & Gifford assisting." Brewer MS, Murray to [Croker], n.d.: "When Mr G[ifford] calls upon you which he will about Brougham's Speech for our next. . ." Smiles II, 48-49 and note: Monk, Gifford, Canning, Croker. Clark 242-43, and 178: "does not sound like Gifford's. He must have turned it [Monk's article] over entirely to Canning and Croker." Brightfield 215-16 and 455: Monk, Canning, Croker, Gifford.

   MONK, JAMES HENRY. *Gentleman's* XXI, 141: Monk

   CANNING, GEORGE. Marriott 146: "inspired by Canning." Dudley 215 and note: "The conclusion surely must be Canning's"

   MONK, JAMES HENRY, and CANNING, GEORGE. Greville I, 74 and note: Monk and Canning; not Dr Ireland

Volume XXI, Number 41 (January 1819)
Published in May 1819: Murray Reg.

493. Article 1. Bristed—Statistical View of America
JACOB, WILLIAM. Murray Reg.: "W. Jacob Senr." *See also* Southey 402

494. Article 2. Wilkins's Translation of Vitruvius
? WILKINS, WILLIAM. Murray Reg.: "—Wilkins." Though Murray Reg. suggests that Wilkins is here reviewing his own book, passages in the article furnish grounds for doubt: see especially *QR* XXI, p. 40

495. Article 3. Gisborne's Natural Theology
WHITAKER, THOMAS DUNHAM. Murray Reg. Nichols xxix

496. Article 4. Abel's Journey in China
BARROW, JOHN. Murray Reg.

497. Article 5. Antiquities of Nursery Literature
COHEN, FRANCIS. Murray Reg. Palgrave

498. Article 6. Bowdler's Select Pieces, in Prose and Verse
IMPEY, JOHN. Murray Reg.: "—Impey."

499. Article 7. Fearon's Sketches of America
BARROW, JOHN. Murray Reg. *See also* Southey 402

500. Article 8. Bentham's Church-of-Englandism
GIFFORD, WILLIAM. Murray Reg.: "Wm Gifford mainly."

501. Article 9. Marsden's Marco Polo
BARROW, JOHN. Murray Reg.

502. Article 10. Inquiry into the Copyright Act
SOUTHEY, ROBERT. Murray Reg. Morgan MS, Southey to Croker, September 16, 1818: "For your next number [of *QR*] I shall have the Churches and Catacombs,—and the Copy right case." Cottle 242-43. Southey 577. *Gentleman's* XXI, 578. *See also* Smiles II, 43; Warter III, 90, 96, 99, 119-20; Southey 368

503. Article 11. Ross's Voyage of Discovery
BARROW, JOHN. Murray Reg. *Gentleman's* XXI, 578

Volume XXI, Number 42 (April 1819)
Published in September: Murray Reg.

504. Article 1. Schlegel's Lectures on Literature
MITCHELL, THOMAS. Murray Reg. *See also D N B*

505. Article 2. De Humboldt's Travels
BARROW, JOHN. Murray Reg. *Gentleman's* XXI, 578

506. Article 3. Hawkins on Tradition
WHATELY, RICHARD. Murray Reg.: "Rev. Whateley."

507. Article 4. Cemeteries and Catacombs of Paris

SOUTHEY, ROBERT. Murray Reg. Murray MS, Gifford to Murray, postmarked Ramsgate, August 6, [1818]: "I expect most from his [Southey's]
Churches & Catacombs—This is just the subject for his peculiar powers."
Morgan MS, Southey to Croker, September 16, 1818: "For your next
number I shall have the Churches and Catacombs . . ." Murray MS, Gifford to Murray, [1819]: "Hayti [see Entry 509] I will set about immediately.—I liked Southey very well; as I read him from end to end in the
Revise. I could not make it shorter." Cottle 242-43. Southey 577, and
401: "That I received them [i.e. some books], you would probably infer
from the mention of Fisher Ames in the Quarterly Review [cf. *QR* XXI,
381]." Warter III, 145-46. Surtees 291, footnote. *Gentleman's* XXI, 578.
See also Smiles II, 43; Warter III, 96; Southey 368

508. Article 5. State of the Laws of Great Britain

MILLER, JOHN. Murray Reg.: "J Miller Linc[oln's] Inn." "Miller" was
written in black ink; the "J" and "Linc Inn" were added in pencil. Murray
MS, Gifford to Murray, Ryde, July 6, 1819: "I think . . . we agreed that
Miller should follow [Gifford had just mentioned Southey, Entry 507, and
Humboldt, Entry 505]—if so let him be set up from the revise which he
has sent, & which I will correct in the proper paging—though I corrected
the ms."

509. Article 6. Past and Present State of Hayti

BARROW, JOHN. Murray Reg. Murray MS, Gifford to Murray, Ryde,
July 6, 1819: "Mr B has sent me . . . Hayti. It makes 20 pages I see. I
have not yet opened or looked at the article." Murray MS, Gifford to
Murray, [1819]: "Hayti I will set about immediately."

510. Article 7. Shelley's Revolt of Islam

COLERIDGE, JOHN TAYLOR. Murray Reg. Brewer MS, Murray to
[Croker], n.d.: "I send you a most extraordinary Poem by Godwins now
Son-in-law—pray keep it under Lock & Key—it is an avowed defense of
Incest—the author is the vilest wretch in existence—living with Leigh
Hunt—The Book was published & he is now endeavouring to suppress it."
Murray MS, Gifford to Murray, Ramsgate, postmarked August 4, 1818:
"By all means, let Mr Coleridge give us a few pages on Shelley." Murray
MS, Gifford to Murray, Ryde, July 6, 1819: ". . . Coleridge's two mss
which he has revised at my desire . . . should be set up as Rowarth has
types . . ." Byron II, 178 and note. Graham 22 and 41. Graham in *SP*
XXII, 504. White 125, 133, 364, 393. *See also* Clark 232, and 276 note
200; Smiles II, 324; Southey 390-91 and note; Simmons 165-66; Bowles
356-66; Milman 80-81
HEBER, REGINALD. Clark 276 note 200. *See also* Clark 232

511. Article 8. Parnell's Maurice and Berghetta

CROKER, JOHN WILSON. Murray Reg. Murray MS, Gifford to Murray,
Ryde, July 19, 1819: "Our friend Croker grows sick of L. Hunt. . . he will
say something on Parnel." Notation on letter: "QR 42." Brightfield 455
CROKER, JOHN WILSON, and GIFFORD, WILLIAM. Clark 199-200:
possibly written by Croker, with touches added by Gifford

512. Article 9. Poems of the Italians; Whistlecraft and Rose

FOSCOLO, UGO. Murray Reg. Murray MS, Gifford to Murray, Ryde, July
6, 1819: ". . . the great question is what we shall do with Foscolo. He
has written a most earnest & pressing entreaty that his Art. may not be
divided. He evidently has set his heart upon it . . . but what can we do?
It makes 90 pages—if I could even reduce it to 75 or 80—& that will make
him wince—still there will be 5 sheets.—Think of this & tell me what

you advise." The article extends pp. 486-556 in *QR*. Murray MS, Gifford to Murray, [1819]: "I send a little of Foscolo to break up into pages . . . He must, I suppose, have a copy, which may then be given to *Cohen* . . ." Smiles II, 52. Eichler 114 and note, and 164 and note. *Gentleman's* XXI, 578. Graham 41. *See also* Smiles II, 8, 13; Grierson V, 168 and note; XII, 433-34; Lockhart V, 100-101 and note

Volume XXII, Number 43 (July 1819)
Published in November: Murray Reg.

513. Article 1. Abernethy etc. on Theories of Life

D'OYLY, GEORGE. Murray Reg. Murray MS, Gifford to Murray, Ryde, July 6, 1819: ". . . D'Oyly . . . may be set up . . . he has taken pains—but I cannot correct it in his close writing." Murray MS, D'Oyly to Murray, [1819]: ". . . a parcel . . . will contain the article I have been preparing on Laurence, Rennell, etc., and all the books. There will be wanting about a page at the end of the article, which I will send from the country in a day or two, not having quite time to conclude it before I leave." D'Oyly 25. *See also* Levy 88-89 and note

514. Article 2. Dupin's Marine Establishments of France and England

BARROW, JOHN. Murray Reg. *Gentleman's* XXI, 578

515. Article 3. Fosbrooke's British Monachism

SOUTHEY, ROBERT. Murray Reg. Cottle 242-43. Southey 577. Warter III, 160. *Gentleman's* XXI, 578. *See also* Heber I, 474-75 and note; Warter III, 138, 141, 145-46; Robinson I, 237

516. Article 4. Ensor's Radical Reform: Restoration of Usurped Rights

JACOB, WILLIAM. Murray MS, Gifford to Murray, Ryde, July 6, 1819: "I send also a little thing of Jacob on Ensor which will not make five pages . . ."
GREY, CHARLES EDWARD. Murray Reg.: "Sir C Grey."

517. Article 5. Golownin's Captivity in Japan

BARROW, JOHN. Murray Reg.

518. Article 6. Woodhouse's Astronomy

BRINKLEY, JOHN. Murray Reg.: "Dr Binckley."

519. Article 7. Knight's Eastern Sketches

CANNING, STRATFORD, Murray Reg.: "Stratd Canning."

520. Article 8. Hazlitt's Political Essays

? GIFFORD, WILLIAM. Graham 41: Gifford. Graham in *SP* XXII, 507 and note: Gifford. Clark 198 and 216-17: Gifford. *See also* Clark 187, and 273 note 98; Robinson I, 237
JACOB, EDWARD. Murray Reg.: "Jacob junr."

521. Article 9. Hill's Ancient Greece; Female Society in Greece

MITCHELL, THOMAS. Murray Reg. Smiles II, 20, and 103 footnote. *DNB*
? FRERE, JOHN HOOKHAM. Robinson I, 237: ". . . probably by Frere"
? SANDFORD, DANIEL KEYTE. *Gentleman's* XXI, 578

522. Article 10. Cape of Good Hope: Emigration
BARROW, JOHN. Murray Reg. *Gentleman's* XXI, 578

523. Article 11. Cottu's Criminal Law in England
CROKER, JOHN WILSON. Murray Reg.: "J W Croker." Addit. note: "not mentioned in Mr Croker's own list." Brightfield 455

Volume XXII, Number 44 (January 1820)
Published in March: Murray Reg.

524. Article 1. Bowdich's Mission to Ashantee
BARROW, JOHN. Murray Reg.

525. Article 2. Stephens's Thesaurus Graecae Linguae
BLOMFIELD, CHARLES JAMES. Murray Reg. Murray MS, Gifford to Murray, n.d.: "I sent Ashantee to begin with last night. I have nothing from Blomfield this morning—this is trifling with us." Murray MS, Gifford to Murray, n.d.: "Mr Blomfield has sent three or four pages more . . ." Blomfield I, 27. *Gentleman's* XXI, 578. *CHEL* XII, 526

526. Article 3. Popular Mythology of the Middle Ages
COHEN, FRANCIS. Murray Reg. Palgrave. *See also* Smiles II, 15

527. Article 4. Strategics—The Archduke Charles
HAY, ROBERT WILLIAM. Murray Reg.

528. Article 5. Payne's Brutus and Shiel's Evadne
COLERIDGE, JOHN TAYLOR. Murray Reg. Graham 41

529. Article 6. De Humboldt's Passage of Himalaya Mountains
BARROW, JOHN. Murray Reg. *Gentleman's* XXI, 578

530. Article 7. Lysias's Letter to the Prince Regent
GRANT, ROBERT. Murray Reg. Smiles II, 52

531. Article 8. Burckhardt's Travels in Nubia
BARROW, JOHN. Murray Reg. Murray MS, Gifford to Murray, n.d.: "Mr Barrow says he is hard at work on Burckhardt's Travels." *Gentleman's* XXI, 578

532. Article 9. Jerome Buonaparte—Court of Westphalia
CROKER, JOHN WILSON. Murray Reg. Murray MS, Gifford to Murray, [February 16, 1820]: "What is become of Mr Croker's Art? It has not been sent to me, & I rather think we shall want it . . ." Brightfield 455

533. Article 10. State of Public Affairs
GRANT, ROBERT. Murray Reg. Murray MS, Gifford to Murray, [February 16, 1820]: "I have nobody to send to Mr Grant—be good enough to let some careful person take the enclosed. This moment I have recd a little more m.s. & the remr is promised tomorrow. I think this Art will make a great impression. Three such magnificent Speeches have never been placed at the head of one before. The extracts are uncommonly fine, & in one place, I must make an addition; but it will be the most striking part of Mr Canning's speech, which as now given reads very abrupt." Murray MS, Gifford to Murray, [February 25, 1820]: "Just after the boy

had gone, the revise reached me from [Gifford leaves blank: possibly Canning?]. Have the goodness to send it to Rowarth that he may go on with it as fast as possible." Smiles II, 52. Clark 178: Gifford added selection from Canning's speech.
SOUTHEY, ROBERT. *Gentleman's* XXI, 578

Volume XXIII, Number 45 (May 1820)

534. Article 1. Coxe's Life of Marlborough

SOUTHEY, ROBERT. Murray Reg. Murray MS, Gifford to Murray, postmarked Ramsgate, August 6, [1818]: "Let him [Southey] take Coxe— This is quite in his way, & he will do it well." Morgan MS, Southey to Croker, Sept. 16, 1818: "For your next number [of *QR*] I shall have the Churches and Catacombs,—and the Copy right case. Next to them a Life of Marlborough concocted from Coxe." Cottle 242-43. Southey 577. Catalogue of the British Museum. *Gentleman's* XXI, 578. *See also* Southey 317, 371, 377, 379; Smiles II, 43; Warter III, 123, 164, 169

535. Article 2. Michael Howe's Van Dieman's Land—The Bush Ranger

FIELD, BARRON. Murray Reg.

536. Article 3. Forbin's Voyage dans le Lavant

BARROW, JOHN. Murray Reg.

537. Article 4. Roads and Highways

BERENS, EDWARD. Murray Reg.: "E Berens." Addit. note: "See E B's letter March 1825."

538. Article 5. De Bosset and Duval on Parga and the Ionian Isles

BARROW, JOHN. Murray Reg.

539. Article 6. Coray's Decline and Corruption of the Greek Tongue

? BLOMFIELD, CHARLES JAMES. Murray Reg.: "By Blomfield." Addit. note: "? Robt. Walpole. See his letter May 1820."
? WALPOLE, ROBERT. See Addit. note under Blomfield

540. Article 7. Voltaire and Madame du Châtelet

CROKER, JOHN WILSON. Murray Reg. Brightfield 455

541. Article 8. Clare's Poems

GILCHRIST, OCTAVIUS GRAHAM. Murray Reg. Graham 41. Clark 273, note 108
SOUTHEY, ROBERT. *Gentleman's* XXI, 578

542. Article 9. Rubichon's De L'Angleterre

CHENEVIX, RICHARD. Murray Reg.

543. Article 10. Milman's Fall of Jerusalem

HEBER, REGINALD. Murray Reg. Grierson VI, 170-71 and note. *Gentleman's* XXI, 578. Graham 41. *See also* Heber I, 420; II, 5; Grierson VI, 177

544. Article 11. Mollien's Course of the Niger

BARROW, JOHN. Murray Reg. *Gentleman's* XXI, 578

545. Article 12. D'Israeli's Manners of the Athenians

MITCHELL, THOMAS. Murray Reg. Graham 41. *DNB*

Volume XXIII, Number 46 (July 1820)
Published in October: Murray Reg.

546. Article 1. Translation of the Bible: Bellamy, Burges, Todd, Whitaker
D'OYLY, GEORGE. Murray Reg.
GOODHUGH, WILLIAM. *Gentleman's* XXI, 578. *DNB*

547. Article 2. Modern Greece: Douglas, Holland, Haygarth
BARROW, JOHN. Murray Reg.

548. Article 3. Parnell's Reply to Quarterly Review
CROKER, JOHN WILSON. Murray Reg. Murray MS, Gifford to Murray, [Summer or early autumn 1820]: "Pray . . . remembrances to Mr Croker & thank him for his Art." The expression "his Art." could refer to Entry 548, to Entry 555, or to Entry 556. Brightfield 455
CROKER, JOHN WILSON, and GIFFORD, WILLIAM. Clark 199-200: Possibly written by Croker with touches added by Gifford

549. Article 4. Grece and Stuart's Emigration to Canada
WHATELY, RICHARD. Murray Reg. Murray MS, Gifford to Murray, [Summer or early autumn 1820]: "Is it possible to let Mr Whately see the revise of Canada? He is at Oriel College." Whately 211 and note

550. Article 5. Spence's Anecdotes of Books and Men
D'ISRAELI, ISAAC. Murray Reg. Murray MS, Gifford to Murray, postmarked Ramsgate, [Summer 1820]: "I hope you will bring Mr D'Israeli's revise . . . as I am stopped." Smiles II, 53. Greever 119 note, and 127. Graham 41. *DNB. CBEL* III, 201. *See also* Grierson VI, 310 note, and 311; Greever 120
CROKER, JOHN WILSON. *Gentleman's* XXI, 578

551. Article 6. Society in Germany by Hodgkin, Jacob and Sand
HAY, ROBERT WILLIAM. Murray Reg. Murray MS, Gifford to Murray, postmarked Ramsgate, August 23, [1820]: "I have but one copy of the Germany, & thought I had desired you to let Mr Hay have yours. . . . Pray send him a revise. I can still improve it a little by a trifling omission & correction or two." Murray MS, Gifford to Murray, Ramsgate, [1820]: "Mr Hay, I suppose will let you have his revise. I hope he will bear the abridgement well. I have certainly done him a kindness. . . There is yet a trifle to take out—but I wait for his papers."

552. Article 7. John Matthews's La Fontaine's Fables
MATTHEWS, HENRY. Murray Reg.

553. Article 8. E D Clarke's Gas Blowpipe
CLARKE, EDWARD DANIEL. Murray Reg.

554. Article 9. Mitchell's Translations of Aristophanes
FRERE, JOHN HOOKHAM. This article is signed at the end with the single letter: W,—perhaps for Frere's pseudonym Whistlecraft. Murray Reg.: "J H Frere." Cites unspecified old letters. Addit. note: "J H Frere's sole article in QR." Murray MS, Gifford to Murray, [Sept or Oct 1820]: "I am a great deal embarrassed about Aristophanes. . . . the light matter . . . though very good, seems out of place in our Review.... yet what will Frere say to cutting out four pages of what he probably considers very highly! And yet, if it must be done, it must." Frere I, 177-79 and notes, and II, 178-214. *QR* XXXII, 45 and note. Eichler 52 and note. *DNB. See also* Frere III, 39 note

555. Article 10. Advice to Julia

CROKER, JOHN WILSON. Murray Reg. Murray MS, Gifford to Murray, [Summer or early autumn 1820]: see Entry 548. Brightfield 455

556. Article 11. Memoirs of R L Edgeworth

CROKER, JOHN WILSON. Murray Reg. Brewer MS, Murray to Croker, n.d.: "Rely upon my silence about E[dgeworth]—you will do a service by taking it out of the hand of Southey who is decided for praising them—but extract what is really interesting too—I will send Sewards Life of Darwin [cf. *QR* XXIII, 534] & any other thing that occur to us . . . your present undertaking will be inserted the moment it shall be received—by the way would not the slight apology with wch you proposed to *open* the Article on E—come with effect at the End—lead the Reader in—not knowing what he is to expect—& convince him—but do [not?] erect his bristles against you at first. . ." Murray MS, Gifford to Murray, [Sept or Oct 1820]: "I saw our friend [Croker?] yesterday—he has his reasons for wishing Edgeworth to appear . . ." Murray MS, Gifford to Murray, [1820]: "I have written to Croker . . . he will be mortified by the omission of his Art.—he talks of having some *personal object* &—what can be done?" Graham 41. Brightfield 455. *See also* Grierson V, 25, footnote, and VI, 95, footnote

557. Article 12. New Churches

SOUTHEY, ROBERT. Murray Reg. Murray MS, Gifford to Murray [Sept or Oct 1820]: "This affair of Southey is a sad one—I never saw his revise. What I had was that which is now printed, from his first proof, so long ago. . . . we cannot do without the Church Art." Cottle 242-43. Southey 577. *Gentleman's* XXI, 578. *See also* Smiles II, 43, 109, 110; Warter III, 96, 99, 122-23, 164-65, 167, 169, 190; Southey 379

Volume XXIV, Number 47 (October 1820)
Published in December: Murray Reg.

558. Article 1. Southey's Life of Wesley

HEBER, REGINALD. Murray Reg. Murray MS, Gifford to Murray, [erroneously dated by another hand: "? June 1821." Probably late 1820]: "Wesley was finished last night, and I sent the whole with the exception of the 1st sheet which had gone before to Hodnet [Heber's residence]. . . . Wesley is very long, but it is written with great care—I shall be able to do something to it after I get it back. I suppose we may begin with it." Heber II, 39. *Gentleman's* XXI, 578. Graham 41. *See also* Heber II, 5

559. Article 2. Wentworth—Oxley. New South Wales

BARROW, JOHN. Murray Reg.

560. Article 3. Italian Tragedy: Manzoni, Foscolo, Pellico

MILMAN, HENRY HART. Murray Reg. Murray MS, Gifford to Murray [erroneously dated "? June 1821." Probably late 1820]: "Milman is now drying at my fire. I shall not read it till Friday. . . I will send a proof to Reading." Milman 75

561. Article 4. Fraser's Himala Mountains

BARROWS, JOHN. Murray Reg.

562. Article 5. Mrs. Hemans's Poems

COLERIDGE, JOHN TAYLOR. Murray Reg. Murray MS, Gifford to
Murray, [summer or early autumn 1820]: "I shall set up that part of Mr
Coleridge which relates to Mrs Hemans . . ." Wales MS, Southey to
Wynn, December 24, 1820: attributes the article to John Coleridge

563. Article 6. Belzoni's Discoveries in Egypt

BARROW, JOHN. Murray Reg. *See also Gentleman's* XXI, 578, which says
this article was compiled from documents sent by Mr Salt

564. Article 7. Burrows's Inquiries Relative to Insanity

UWINS, DAVID. Murray Reg.: "Dr Ewens." *Gentleman's* XXI, 578

565. Article 8. Committee on Criminal Laws

MILLER, JOHN. Murray Reg.: "—— Miller."

Volume XXIV, Number 48 (January 1821)
Published in April: Murray Reg.

566. Article 1. Freedom of Commerce: Liverpool's Speech

FLETCHER [possibly M. Fletcher of London]. Murray Reg.: "——Fletcher."

567. Article 2. Maturin's Melmoth the Wanderer

CROKER, JOHN WILSON. Murray Reg. Murray MS, Gifford to Murray, [January 25, 1821]: "Croker's little Art is exceedingly good, & Barrows much more amusing than you led me to expect. It wants to be [cut?]
by a friendly hand, and this I cannot lend it for a day or two." Graham
41. Brightfield 455. *See also* Clark 199: Its form, but not its irony, is
very much like Gifford's.

568. Article 3. Murray's Asiatic Discoveries

BARROW, JOHN. Murray Reg. Murray MS, Gifford to Murray, [January
25, 1821]: "Crokers little Art is exceeding good, & Barrows much more
amusing than you led me to expect. It wants to be [cut?] by a friendly
hand, and this I cannot lend it for a day or two."

569. Article 4. Accum on Culinary Poisons

MACCULLOCH, JOHN. Murray Reg.: "Dr McCulloch."

570. Article 5. Modern Novels—Austen's Northanger Abbey & Persuasion

WHATELY, RICHARD. Murray Reg.: "Sir W Scott." Cites unspecified
old letters. Addit. note: "by Dr Whateley—from Lockhart's Life of Scott
in wh book, however, it is inserted by mistake." Murray MS, Gifford to
Murray, [January 25, 1821]: "Have you recd, any parcel for me from
Cheltenham? Mr Whately promised to send one, & actually sent it a week
ago." Lockhart VI, 187 note. Whately pp. iii-iv and 282. *Gentleman's*
XXI, 578. Tuckwell 55. *QR* CCX, 740. Graham 41-42. Reitzel in *PMLA*
XLIII, 487. Hogan in *PMLA* XLV, 1265-66 and note: Probably "doctored"
by Gifford. Keynes 245, item 257. Bonnell 371 and note. *CHEL* XII,
490. *CBEL* III, 383. *See also* Scott. However, Lockhart VI, 187 note,
corrects the mistake

571. Article 6. Barker's Aristarchus Anti-Blomfieldianus

MONK, JAMES HENRY. Murray Reg. Blomfield I, 27-28. *See also* Blomfield I, 34-35

572. Article 7. Rise and Progress of Horticulture

LOUDON, JOHN CLAUDIUS. Murray Reg.: "C. J. Loudon." Murray MS, Gifford to Murray, postmarked July 19, 1822: "Some one has sent me a review of a horticultural work by Loudon. Can this be our quondam friend? If so, I am sorry for him, for he appears, from the quotations to be an ignorant, imprudent & even profligate scribbler. I was well aware from his Art that he could not write at all; but I gave him credit for knowledge of his subject & therefore took pains with his paper, which contained many curious facts."

573. Article 8. Manners of the Athenians

MITCHELL, THOMAS. Murray Reg. *DNB*

574. Article 9. Huntington's Works and Life

SOUTHEY, ROBERT. Murray Reg. Cottle 242-43. Southey 577. *Gentleman's* XXI, 578. Huchon 217 note. *See also* Southey 387 note; Smiles II, 110; Warter III, 216, 225

575. Article 10. Hope's Anastasius

MATTHEWS, HENRY. Murray Reg.
GIFFORD, WILLIAM. *Gentleman's* XXI, 578. Graham 41. Clark 193: This article "is similar in method to Gifford's other articles." *See also* Clark 187 and 273, note 98

576. Article 11. Madame de Genlis: Petrarque et Laure

FOSCOLO, UGO. Murray Reg. Wicks 35: Mutilated. *See also* Wicks 17; Moore III, 293, 329

Volume XXV, Number 49 (April 1821)
Published in June: Murray Reg.

577. Article 1. Spanish Drama

MILMAN, HENRY HART. Murray Reg.
SOUTHEY, ROBERT. *Gentleman's* XXI, 578

578. Article 2. Lyon's Northern Africa and the Niger

BARROW, JOHN. Murray Reg. *Gentleman's* XXI, 578

579. Article 3. Sketch Book, by Washington Irving

MATTHEWS, HENRY. Murray Reg. Murray MS, Gifford to Murray, [erroneously dated "? June 1821." Probably late 1820]: "If our friend Matthews does not give us a much better review of the Sketchbook than theirs [*The Edinburgh Review's*], I will, without ceremony, fling it into the fire." Pencil notation on letter "QR 49." Murray MS, Gifford to Murray, [n.d.]: "I enclose to you the letter for our friend Matthews as I know not whether he lives with his father, or where to find him. . . . Belmont . . . is all my direction. . ." Graham 41 (Graham erroneously locates this article in No. 50). Clark 239 (Clark erroneously locates this article in No. 50).

580. Article 4. Dupin's Military Force of Great Britain

PROCTER, GEORGE. Murray Reg.: "Capt Proctor"

581. Article 5. The Etonian. Nos I-VII

WALKER, WILLIAM SIDNEY. Murray Reg.: "Rev—Walker."

582. Article 6. Normandy—Architecture of the Middle Ages

COHEN, FRANCIS. Murray Reg. Palgrave

583. Article 7. Galt's Annals of the Parish

CROKER, JOHN WILSON. Murray Reg. Brewer MS, Murray to [Croker], n.d.: "I hope you will send the Annals of the Parish to Aristarchus [Gifford?] as we have a place for fitting it in immediately—and your obliging communication on the other book I long to send you a compleat revise of." Graham 41. Brightfield 455

584. Article 8. Mitford's History of Greece, Vol. V

HAYGARTH, WILLIAM. Murray Reg.: "Haygarth."

585. Article 9. Parry's Voyage of Discovery

BARROW, JOHN. Murray Reg. *Gentleman's* XXI, 578. *See also* Warter III, 261

586. Article 10. Scudamore on Mineral Waters

Author not identified

587. Article 11. Fergusson's Decisions in Actions of Divorce

GLASSFORD, JAMES. Murray Reg.: "Jas Glassford (Edinboro)." Murray MS, Gifford to Murray, [Sept 1820]: "Do not forget Southey, nor our Edinbg correspondent—for we must not lose any friends. His address is James Glassford, 52 Castle Str. Edinburgh . . ."

Volume XXV, Number 50 (July 1821)
Published in October: Murray Reg.

588. Article 1. Life of Cromwell

SOUTHEY, ROBERT. Murray Reg. Murray MS, Gifford to Murray, Ramsgate, [July 19, 1821]: "I have recd both Southey & Mrs Hemans . . . Southey has contrived to tell a wretched tale of blood & guilt in the homeliest of all possible ways. I never read so dry and uninviting a stile, twill not go down. But keep this to yourself." Murray MS, Gifford to Murray, James Street, Wednesday night [1821]: "Southey's conclusion may perhaps have lost a little spirit but I saw nothing so valuable in the two paragraphs as to make one wish to retain them & they might, as you think, have at this time given displeasure." British Museum MS, Southey to Peachey, Aug 23, 1821: ". . . when I have told you that you will see a sketch of Oliver Cromwell's life in the next number of Q R you will have l[earned? Seal torn out] as much of my occupation as is worth communicating." Cottle 242-43. Southey 577 and 404: "Gifford has made only one alteration . . ." Warter III, 283 and 284-85. Smiles II, 39. Rickman 218-19. *Gentleman's* XXI, 578. Clark 181 and 272, note 64. *See also* Smiles II, 109, 110; Warter III, 216, 254, 256, 261; *D N B* in article on Gifford

589. Article 2. Hone's Apocryphal New Testament

ROSE, HUGH JAMES. Murray Reg.: "Rev H Rose." Rose XI, 388. *Gentleman's* XXI, 578. *DNB*

590. Article 3. De Humboldt's Personal Narrative

BARROW, JOHN. Murray Reg. Murray MS, Gifford to Murray, postmarked Ramsgate, [July] 1821: "I send a little parcel containing the revise of Humboldt for Rowarth, a sheet for press, and the first part of Humboldt for Mr Barrow, as I suppose he would like to see it. . . . I fancy I shall be able to improve this sheet when it returns to me. . . . our friend has been somewhat too rapid."

591. Article 4. Lord Waldegrave's Memoirs

CROKER, JOHN WILSON. Murray Reg. Murray MS, Gifford to Murray, postmarked Ramsgate, [July] 1821: "I suppose we may follow Humboldt with Mr Croker's clever paper on Waldegrave." *Gentleman's* XXI, 578. Brightfield 455

592. Article 5. Staunton's Embassy to the Tourgouth Tartars

BARROW, JOHN. Murray Reg.

593. Article 6. J H Hunt's Tasso's Jerusalem Delivered

HEBER, REGINALD. Murray Reg. Murray MS, Gifford to Murray, n.d.: "Our friend Heber has sent me by this morning's post a short review of Hunt's translation of Tasso—not our friend Leigh H but a country clergyman of that unfortunate name. It is not all written by himself [Heber?] but tis smart enough." Notation on letter: "QR 50." Murray MS, Gifford to Murray, Ramsgate, n.d.: "I think, too, we must have Heber's Tasso. I have gone over it very carefully." Graham 41. Clark 217. *See also* Heber I, 486; Warter III, 282-83

594. Article 7. Martyn's Memoir—Religious Missions

GILLY, WILLIAM. Murray Reg.: "Rev W Gilly (Wanstead)"

595. Article 8. Cape of Good Hope

BARROW, JOHN. Murray Reg. Warter III, 282-83, when read with *QR* XXV, p. 466, on fertility of the region

596. Article 9. Report on the State of Agriculture

SENIOR, NASSAU WILLIAM. Murray MS, Gifford to Murray, franked August 15, 1821: "Just as I had finished this sentence, the coach brought me Mr Senior's ms. It is bulky but if it answers the importance of the subject that will be no evil." Seymour 242-43. *DNB.* Levy 97-105, 110, 367. *See also* Ricardo-Trower 168

597. Article 10. Blomfield's Aeschylus's Agamemnon

SYMMONS, JOHN. Murray Reg.

598. Article 11. Lady Morgan's Italy

CROKER, JOHN WILSON. Murray Reg. Brightfield 455. *See also* Clark 199: This article contains much that is characteristic of Gifford's writings.

599. Article 12. England and France

CHENEVIX RICHARD. Murray Reg. Murray MS, Gifford to Murray, postmarked Ramsgate, July 18, 1821: ". . . a letter from Mr Chenevix, by which I have the mortification to find that the parcel has miscarried for the second time."
CROKER, JOHN WILSON. *Gentleman's* XXI, 578

Volume XXVI, Number 51 (October 1821)
Published in December: Murray Reg.

600. Article 1. Dupin's Navy of England and France

BARROW, JOHN. Murray Reg. Smiles II, 54 and note

601. Article 2. Russian Church Architecture

WHITTINGTON, ——. Murray Reg.: "Whittington." Murray MS, Gifford to Murray, [December 28, 1821]: "I enclose Mr Whittington's letter which I ought to have given you . . ."

602. Article 3. McQueen's Africa, Niger River and State of Slave Trade

BARROW, JOHN. Murray Reg. Murray MS, Gifford to Murray, [December 28, 1821]: ". . . I have seen that [article in *Edinburgh Review*] on the Slave Trade. A more perfect contrast between the two Revws cannot be found than those two furnish & surely never was triumph more complete . . . as for Barrow! comparison is a jest. One is all & the other nothing. . . . I have read again . . . all of Barrow." Notation on letter: "QR 51 ER 71."

603. Article 4. Copleston and Whately on Predestination

BLOMFIELD, CHARLES JAMES. Murray Reg. Blomfield I, 82

604. Article 5. Hazlitt's Table Talk

MATTHEWS, JOHN. Murray Reg.: "Col. Matthews." Smiles II, 54 and note. Graham 41. Graham in *SP* XXII, 507. Clark 218

605. Article 6. Novels by the Author of "Waverley"

SENIOR, NASSAU WILLIAM. Murray Reg. Brewer MS, Murray to Croker, July 30, Thursday, [1818]: "I have sent for the 'Trials' and I will be glad if you are so obliging as to give us an article on the new Tales, will you venture your thoughts upon the genius and the Art of their author—by which he creates fiction out of reality without injury to historical facts—You may rely with certainty upon S's being the author of at least these and the former *Tales* and of Rob Roy—for his publisher as I told you taking for granted, that, as I published the former Tales, I must be in the secret, told me many conversations about them, with Scott—perhaps out of your ingenuity you can manage to pay him some gratifying compliment—A work which is the subject of universal admiration merits the expenditure of some talent in a review of it." Smiles II, 54 and note. Senior. *Gentleman's* XXI, 578. Seymour 242-43. Brightfield 343. Hillhouse 50. Levy 83 and 363
WHATELY, RICHARD. Graham 41

606. Article 7. Godwin and Malthus on Population

TAYLOR, GEORGE. Surtees xiv

607. Article 8. Shelley's Prometheus Unbound

WALKER, WILLIAM SIDNEY. Murray Reg.: "Rev Walker." *QR* CCX, 756: Mr Walker of Cambridge. Graham 41: "W S Walker." Graham in *SP* XXII, 504: "W S Walker." White 240, 369, 393. *See also* White 310

608. Article 9. Astrology and Alchemy: Moore and Brande

COHEN, FRANCIS. Murray Reg. Smiles II, 53 and 54 and note. Palgrave

609. Article 10. Della-Cella's Route from Tripoli to Egypt

BARROW, JOHN. Murray Reg.

610. Article 11. Morellet's Memoirs of the French Revolution

CROKER, JOHN WILSON. Murray Reg. Smiles II, 54. Brightfield 455

611. Article 12. Dalzel's Lectures on the Ancient Greeks

MITCHELL, THOMAS. Murray Reg. Murray MS, Gifford to Murray, [December 28, 1821]: "I have toiled thru the Greek art in the Edin[*burgh Review*] and a perfect toil it was . . . By way of recovering myself, I have read again three or four beautiful pages of Mitchell. . . ." Notation on letter: "QR 51 ER 71". Murray MS, Gifford to Murray, [1821]: "It was my design to give Mitchell whose paper has much beautiful writing in it." Smiles II, 54 and note. See also Smiles II, 20

Volume XXVI, Number 52 (January 1822)
Published in March: Murray Reg.

612. Article 1. Dobrizhoffer's Account of the Abipones (translated by Sara Coleridge)

SOUTHEY, ROBERT. Murray Reg. Cites unspecified old letters. Cottle 242-43. Southey 577. *See also* Warter III, 286, 289, 301; Southey 404

613. Article 2. Bishop of St David's Vindication of St John

Author not identified

614. Article 3. Kotzebue's Voyage of Discovery

BARROW, JOHN. Murray Reg.: indistinct pencil entry "J Barrow" or "? Barra." *Gentleman's* XXI, 578

615. Article 4. Galt's Memoirs of a Life in Pennsylvania

CROKER, JOHN WILSON. Murray Reg. Cites unspecified old letters. Brightfield 455

616. Article 5. Buckingham's Travels in Palestine

BANKES, WILLIAM JOHN. Murray Reg.: indistinct pencil entry "? W J Bankes." Addit. note: "Apparently Mr. Bankes was sued by Buckingham in consequence of this article. See Bankes letter to J M June 29, 1826 (Sape [i.e. in safe?])." *Gentleman's* XXI, 578. *DNB*: Bankes inspired or wrote it.

617. Article 6. Arrowsmith on Instructing Infant Deaf and Dumb

Author not identified

618. Article 7. Mémoires du Duc de Lauzun

CROKER, JOHN WILSON. Murray Reg. Cites unspecified old letters. Brightfield 455

619. Article 8. Harmon's Journal of Voyages and Travels in North America

Author not identified

620. Article 9. Weights and Measures

Author not identified

621. Article 10. Memoirs of the Kit-Cat Club

CROKER, JOHN WILSON. Murray Reg. Cites unspecified old letters. Brightfield 455
? GIFFORD, WILLIAM (in part). Clark 199: Gifford may have had a hand in writing it

622. Article 11. Ker Porter's Travels in Georgia and Persia

Author not identified

623. Article 12. The Pirate, by the Author of Waverly

SENIOR, NASSAU WILLIAM. Lockhart VI, 179-80. Senior 76-96. *Gentleman's* XXI, 578. Graham 41. Hillhouse 50

624. Article 13. Dugald Stewart's Second Dissertation

Author not identified. *See*, however, *Gentleman's* XXI, 578, where two names are mentioned: Dr Sayers and Mr Bowdler. But Dr Frank Sayers and John Bowdler the Younger, both dead, are out of the question. Thomas Bowdler the Shakespeare critic lived until 1825

625. Article 14. Malte-Brun's Spurious Voyages

BARROW, JOHN. Murray Reg. Addit. note: "See letter from J B   Nov 26/21"

626. Article 14. Colonial Policy

Author not identified

Volume XXVII, Number 53 (April 1822)
Published in July: Murray Reg.

627. Article 1. Life and Writings of Camoëns: Adamson and Macedo

SOUTHEY, ROBERT. Murray Reg. Cites unspecified old letters. Cottle 242-43. Southey 577. *Gentleman's* XXI, 579. *See also* Smiles II, 110; Warter III, 289, 295

628. Article 2. History of the Aeolic Digamma: Granville Penn

FOSCOLO, UGO. Murray Reg. Cites unspecified old letters. Smiles II, 137. Wicks 42. *Gentleman's* XXI, 579

629. Article 3. Tour of North America: Harris, Welby and Flower

Author not identified

630. Article 4. Evans's VanDiemen's Land

Author not identified

631. Article 5. Reid on Nervous Affections

GOOCH, ROBERT. Lucas II, 408 note: "supposed to be [by] Dr Gooch." Clark 225 and 277 and note 227

632. Article 6. Copyright—Cases of Walcot v. Walker, etc.

SENIOR, NASSAU WILLIAM. Levy 106-10
SOUTHEY, ROBERT. *Gentleman's* XXI, 579

633. Article 7. Nazaroff's Expedition to Kokania

Author not identified

634. Article 8. Montlosier—De la Monarchie Française

Author not identified

635. Article 9. Walpole's Memoirs of Reign of George II

CROKER, JOHN WILSON. Murray Reg. Cites unspecified old letters. *Gentleman's* XXI, 579. Jennings I, 249 and note. Brightfield 455

636. Article 10. Waddington's Visit to Ethiopia

Author not identified

637. Article 11. State of the Currency

COPLESTON, EDWARD. Ricardo-Malthus 212 and note. Copleston 347. *Gentleman's* XXI, 579. *See also* Dudley 312, 315, 322 and note, 333

Volume XXVII, Number 54 (July 1822)
Published in October: Murray Reg.

638. Article 1. Bankes's Early History of Rome

HAYGARTH, WILLIAM. Murray Reg.: "Wm Haygarth." Cites unspecified old letters. Addit. note: "from a letter of W H's."
ARNOLD, THOMAS. *Gentleman's* XXI, 579

639. Article 2. Cottingham's Styles of Architecture

COHEN, FRANCIS. Murray Reg. Murray MS, Gifford to Murray, postmarked Ramsgate, July 13 [or 18], 1822: "Cohen, too, I have read here—Before I left town he requested that the Edinburgh Advertisement might, above all, be preserved. I had not read it. He is very wrong, for the thing is heavy & dull & not a creature will wade through it. It spoils his paper & should not be preserved in it—but I will write him. The article itself is excellent." Murray MS, Gifford to Murray, postmarked Ramsgate, July 27, 1822: "There is also Cohen's Art which I wish him to have as soon as possible. If we can agree about the dull long-winded advertisement, there is nothing to dispute about. He has improved it since I saw it, & the paper is, in fact, highly creditable to his powers of writing..."

640. Article 3. Scott's Fortunes of Nigel

SENIOR, NASSAU WILLIAM. Murray Reg.: "? Nassau Senior" in pencil. Senior 97-137. Levy 97-98. Hillhouse 50

641. Article 4. Campbell's Missionary Travels in South Africa

BARROW, JOHN. Murray Reg. Cites unspecified old letters. Addit. note: "from a letter of J B's July 13 1822." Murray MS, Gifford to Murray, postmarked July 19, 1822: "Barrow says that he has a short paper on Campbell. . ."

642. Article 5. Jeremy Bentham's Art of Packing Juries

Author not identified

643. Article 6. Panegyrical Oratory of Greece: Planche and Abbé Auger

MITCHELL, THOMAS. Murray Reg. Cites unspecified old letters. Murray MS, Gifford to Murray, postmarked July 13 [or 18], 1822: "I have also read Mitchell twice. He is very clever & lively entertaining, & visibly improves. Still he wants tact to govern his feelings & experience of what the world will bear . . . There is a want of connection & a desultory slipping into the midst of modern times while in the height of antient discussion. The paper is far too long as it is, & yet he must say a word or two on the French translation. If he has not read it, send him the Edinb Revw & he may make up something from the extracts which are all that I know of the work. He has not, I suppose, put the last hand to it. When he has done this, let me have his copy, & I will go to work with it—What is cut out may be used hereafter. Upon the whole my judgment of the paper is highly favourable. . . . I once thought that Mr Mitchell . . . might be useful to us in light articles of two or three pages, but I am convinced now that if he is not *great* he is nothing... I like his notion of taking up the Don & Friar much. The latter, I believe is little understood in this country, and therefore, little praised." Murray MS, Gifford to Murray, postmarked Ramsgate, July 19, 1822: "Our friend Mitchell you see, has made the very discovery which my former letter pointed out. Let him by all means, do as he says. But some work must be chosen to head the art. Of the satisfaction I feel at his taking up the Don I spoke before . . . let Mr Mitchell lose no time . . . He has not much [more] to do..." *See also DNB*

644. Article 7. Campaigns in the Canadas : James, Thomson, Sir G. Prevost

PROCTER, GEORGE. Murray Reg: "Geo Procter." Cites unspecified old letters. Addit. note: "from a letter of his own. Feb 16/1822 he had been a soldier (? Major) & writes from R M College." Murray MS, Gifford to Murray, postmarked Ramsgate, July 18, 1821 : "I add a very good letter from Procter. He promises just such a thing as I wish—he knows very little of me if he supposes I want him to spare Sir G. Prevost. Had my advice been taken, the American war would have ended very differently & Barrow knows it." Murray MS, Gifford to Murray, postmarked July 27, 1822 : Gifford says he is sending Procter's revised MS.

645. Article 8. Mayow's Sermons and Miscellanies

Author not identified

646. Article 9. Buckland on Fossil Bones

Author not identified

647. Article 10. Lord Byron's Dramas

HEBER, REGINALD. Murray Reg.: "W Gifford or Bp Heber." Apparently that entry in Murray Reg. first read simply "W Gifford," and an Addit. note explained thus: "authors name given in letter of Sir G. Dallas. Nov 1822." Later, apparently after discovery of conflicting evidence, Murray Reg. was altered to read as it now stands: "W Gifford or Bp Heber"; and the further Addit. note was then given: "Bp Heber. See Byron's Life. 8vo Ed. p. 570 note." Heber II, 59 and note. *Gentleman's* XXI, 579. Graham 41. Clark 207 and 275 note 169

GIFFORD, WILLIAM. Murray Reg.: "W Gifford or Bp Heber." For full details, see explanation above, under Heber

IRELAND, JOHN. Warter III, 348

648. Article 11. Contagion and Quarantine

GOOCH, ROBERT. *Gentleman's* XXI, 579. *Sketches* 140

Volume XXVIII, Number 55 (October 1822)
Published in February 1823 : Murray Reg.

649. Article 1. Grégoire on Religious Sects

SOUTHEY, ROBERT. Murray Reg. Cottle 242-43. Southey 577. *Gentleman's* XXI, 579. *See also* Warter II, 412, and III, 340; Southey 310 and 410

650. Article 2. Sir C. H. Williams's Works

CROKER, JOHN WILSON. Murray Reg. Brightfield 455

651. Article 3. Egypt, Nubia, Berber, and Sennaar

BARROW, JOHN. Murray Reg. *Gentleman's* XXI, 579

652. Article 4. Jouy's Sylla, a Tragedy

COLERIDGE, JOHN TAYLOR. Murray Reg.

653. Article 5. Crawfurd's Indian Archipelago

BARROW, JOHN, and RAFFLES, SIR THOMAS STAMFORD. Murray Reg.: "Sir Stamford Raffles & J. Barrow." Murray MS, Gifford to Murray, postmarked Ramsgate, July 19, 1822 : ". . . he [Barrow] is very anxious for the Art. on Crawford which he & Marden say is sound & good,

I suppose therefore it must be inserted, especially as Sir J [or T?] Raffles is coming home & he expects much assistance from him. The paper is not very brisk, but tis sensible."

654. Article 6. Moore's Irish Melodies

TAYLOR, HENRY. Taylor I, 41-42. *DNB.* Graham 41. Kunitz 605. *See also* Simmons 179

655. Article 7. Whately's Party Feeling in Matters of Religion

Author not identified. Murray MS, Gifford to Murray, postmarked July 19, 1822: "I have received from another unknown hand a good paper on Whately's Bampton Lectures." *See also* Heber II, 86 and 62

656. Article 8. Strangeways' Sketch of the Mosquito Shore & Poyais

BARROW, JOHN. Murray Reg.

657. Article 9. Slave Trade

BARROW, JOHN. Murray Reg.

658. Article 10. Adultery—Prize Essay

Author not identified

659. Article 11. Champollion's Hieroglyphical Alphabet

BARROW, JOHN. Murray Reg.

660. Article 12. The Opposition

ROBINSON, DAVID, and GIFFORD, WILLIAM. Murray Reg.: "All that is excellent by Wm Gifford. David Robinson." Addit. note: "David Robinson nominally author. See his own letter Sep 2/1823/"

661. Article 13. O'Meara's Napoleon in Exile

CROKER, JOHN WILSON. Murray Reg. Murray MS, Gifford to Murray, postmarked July 13 [or 18], 1822: "I have indeed run thru Dr O'Meara . . . A couple of precious scoundrels & saints—the Dr & his patron are! I trust however they are both in Mr Croker's hands whose property they naturally are." Murray MS, Gifford to Murray, [Oct 1822]: "We can hardly have O'Meara for this No. I suppose . . . I own I shall not, unless Mr C expects it, wish to wait. If he is anxious about it, we must, I suppose have it but it will make us very late." Murray MS, Gifford to Murray, [March 1823]: "[A report says] the French have had the Art. on O'Meara translated & dispersed in great numbers about Paris & the country. Our friend seldom writes in vain." Brewer MS, Murray to [Croker], [pencil notation: March 31, 1823]: "I have just seen Mr Wilmot who has undertaken to favour me with an article on O'Meara & when you come back we will give him materials— a Pamphlet, from America, I conceive, is advertised for the 1st of April." Cf. Entry 719. Croker 72 note. *Gentleman's* XXI, 579. Brightfield 455

Volume XXVIII, Number 56 (January 1823)
Published in July: Murray Reg.
Edited, at least in part, by Croker: Smiles II, 57-58

662. Article 1. Lacretelle's The Constituent Assembly

CHENEVIX, RICHARD. Murray Reg. Murray MS, Gifford to Murray, [July, 1823]: see Entry 676
CROKER, JOHN WILSON. *Gentleman's* XXI, 579

663. Article 2. Burton's Antiquities and Curiosities of Rome

BLUNT, JOHN JAMES. Murray Reg.: "Rev T J [or J J?] Blunt."

664. Article 3. Arago—Voyage Round the World

BARROW, JOHN. Murray Reg.

665. Article 4. Chalmers on Poor-Laws

GLEIG, GEORGE, and CROKER, JOHN WILSON. Murray Reg.: "? Mr
Gleig." Murray MS, Gifford to Murray, [1823]: "I found here a Rev of
Chalmers by Dr Gleig . . . I am pleased . . . as he is well able to do it
justice . . . I have not [yet] looked at a word of it . . ." Smiles II, 56-57:
Gleig. Smiles II, 57, quotes Croker's letter to Murray, March 29, 1823:
"I return the *Poor* article [Note says: Gleig's in no. 56] with its additions.
Let the author's amendments be attended to, and let his termination be in-
serted *between* his former conclusion and that which I have written."

666. Article 5. Ducas's Travels in Europe

PROCTER, GEORGE. Murray Reg.: "Capt Proctor."

667. Article 6. Franklin's Polar Seas

BARROW, JOHN. Murray Reg. *Gentleman's* XXI, 579

668. Article 7. Abraham Moore's Pindar

COLERIDGE, JOHN TAYLOR. Murray Reg. Brewer MS, Murray to
[Croker], [pencil notation: March 1823]: ". . . convey to *Mr* GIFFORD the
articles on Pindar & Mr Southeys own on Gregoire." Murray MS, Gifford
to Murray, [March 1823]: "Pray send off by this post Coleridge's Pindar
. . ."

669. Article 8. Navigation Laws

FLETCHER [possibly M. Fletcher of London]. Murray Reg.: "———
Fletcher."

670. Article 9. Madame Campan's Memoirs of Marie-Antoinette

CROKER, JOHN WILSON. Murray Reg. Brewer MS, Murray to [Crok-
er], [pencil notation: June 1823]: I send the 2 articles on Royal Memoirs
[i.e. Entry 670 and Entry 671]. I suspect all but the last page of the first
is worked off, but I will cancel if you find this necessary. Can you send
me the title that you have finally fixed upon for these Royal Memoirs? I
wish to insert it in a List now waiting for it. Croker 72 and note. *Gentleman's* XXI, 579: J W Croker? Brightfield 455. *See also* Smiles II, 58

671. Article 10. Memoirs of the Royal Family of France

CROKER, JOHN WILSON. Murray Reg. Brewer MS, Murray to [Crok-
er], [pencil notation: June 1823]: see Entry 670. Croker 105 and note,
and 241 and note. *Gentleman's* XXI, 579: J W Croker? Brightfield 455

672. Article 11. Cause of the Greeks

HAYGARTH, WILLIAM. Murray Reg.: "Wm Haygarth." Murray MS,
Gifford to Murray, Ramsgate, June 20, [1823]: ". . . I have . . . looked
over Greece, of which I must have a revise . . . I wish the Greece had been
half so soberly written [as Art 13, on Spain, was]." Murray MS, Gifford
to Murray, [July 1823]: "As for Greece, let it go as it is . . . some allow-
ance will be made for its enthusiastic tone—besides I have omitted a good
deal that was objectionable . . . Mr Haygarth is very anxious about its
appearance: so pray indulge him. Some parts of it are very good."

673. Article 12. Progress of Infidelity: Grégorie on Théophilanthropie

SOUTHEY, ROBERT. Murray Reg. Brewer MS, Murray to [Croker],

[pencil notation: March 1823]: ". . . convey to *Mr* GIFFORD the article on Pindar & Mr Southeys own on Gregoire." Murray MS, Gifford to Murray, Ramsgate, June 20 [1823]: ". . . I have . . . looked over . . . as much of Southey as I can find here . . . the conclusion of Infidelity . . . you can get Rowarth to send me without delay." Marginal note: "I have since found Southey." Murray MS, Gifford to Murray, Ramsgate [July 1823]: "Has Southey sent anything? His last is prolix—but I think better of it than Mr Murdock does, & it will do good . . ." British Museum MS, Southey to Peachey, Oct 4, 1823: "In the preceding number [i.e., the one before the last] you would perhaps recognize me upon the Progress of Infidelity,—a paper which underwent some injurious curtailments." Cottle 242-43. Southey 577. Lucas II, 393 and note. Hutchinson I, 289. Rickman 225. *Gentleman's* XXI, 579. *C H E L* XII, 220. Graham in *SP* XXII, 510. Clark 225. Anthony 198. *See also* Smiles II, 58; Warter 340, 386

674. Article 13. Affairs of Spain

HAY, ROBERT WILLIAM. Murray Reg.: "R W Hay." Murray MS, Gifford to Murray, [1823]: ". . . somebody should have an eye to Hay's Art. I suspect that you have been misled & have misled me for I see no trace of its having been revised by any government hand. However, it is safe, though far from elegant or tasty . . . Jacob called here and read it while I was out. He made one or two marginal marks which I shall attend to. He appears . . . to like it." Murray MS, Gifford to Murray, Ramsgate, June 20, [1823]: ". . . I shall send off Spain with the next parcel & not want to see it again . . . I wish the Greece had been half so soberly written." Murray MS, Gifford to Murray, [July 1823]: " I send the remr of Spain. It is not necessary that I should see it again; but Mr H or some one for him, should look at the revise. . . . I have lightened the Art & it will not read amiss. The pencil m.s. at the end is by Mr Jacob, who read it as I believe I told you, in my absence. I have not seen him since." *See also* Warter III, 383

Volume XXIX, Number 57 (April 1823)

Published in September: Murray Reg. Edited in part by Croker, Barrow, and Murray: Brightfield 182 and 353

675. Article 1. Valley of the Mississippi

BARROW, JOHN, and GIFFORD, WILLIAM. Murray Reg.: "J Barrow." Murray MS, Gifford to Murray, Ramsgate, [July 1823]: ". . . I thought Barrow was in forwardness. His Ionia Art would be good to begin with, or if that is not ready, perhaps his America which I suppose is finished." Murray MS, Gifford to Murray, [September 1823]: "Let Mr Barrow have a revise of his Art. He has forgotten all that we have said of America, and is quite full of admiration of the country. I have mentioned it to him, & altered his language—but I must see the Art. again." Murray MS, Gifford to Murray, Ramsgate, [September 1823]: "I return Mr Barrows revise had I not been very ill the last four days, it should have been sent before; but it was not in my power to finish it till late last night . . ." *Gentleman's* XXI, 579: Barrow

676. Article 2. French Tragedy

CHENEVIX, RICHARD. Murray Reg. Murray MS, Gifford to Murray, Ramsgate, [July 1823]: "Have you sent the proofs of Crim Tartary to Mr W. Or the Dramatic papers to Chenevix?—By the way I hear great praise of his last paper [i.e., Entry 662?], & tis certainly beautiful." Murray MS, Gifford to Murray, [September 1823]: "Chenevix I thought of putting into one Art. but the first part, at all events, may be set up." See Entry 689 for the second part of the material

677. Article 3. Southey's Peninsular War

PROCTER, GEORGE, and CROKER, JOHN WILSON. Murray Reg.:
"Captn G. Procter." Smiles II, 57-58. *See also* Warter III, 405

678. Article 4. Goodisson's Ionian Islands

BARROW, JOHN (?Corrected by Canning). Murray Reg.: "J Barrow."
Cites old letters. Three Addit. notes: (1) "from the Notes (signed) of Sir
F Hervey." (2) "? corrected by Mr Canning." (3) "See J Barrows
letter Aug 18/23." Murray MS, Gifford to Murray, Ramsgates, [July
1823]: ". . . I thought Barrow was in forwardness. His Iona Art. would
be good to begin with. . ."

679. Article 5. Manners of the Crim Tartars: Mary Holderness

? WHITTINGTON, ———. Murray Reg.: "?Whittington." The *?* is in
pencil. Murray MS, Gifford to Murray, Ramsgate, [July 1823]: "Have
you sent the proofs of Crim. Tartary to Mr W? Or the Dramatic papers
to Chenevix?"

680. Article 6. Buckland's Reliquiae Diluvianae

COPLESTON, EDWARD. Murray Reg. Addit. note: "Provost of Oriel.
an article was written by Mr Barrow & withdrawn in favour of this one—
See Dr Buckland's letter Feb 3/1823." Murray MS, Gifford to Murray,
Ramsgate, [July 1823]: "Buckland, I know, complains that he has been
treated solely as a geological writer—but he aspires to something higher,
and it was this which made me wish for a more philosophical view of the
subject; and this the Provost could well have given." Murray MS, Gifford to Murray, [July 1823]: "The Provost of Oriel has written to me
this morning to say that he has an Article on Buckland, taking a philosophical view of the subject. This is just what is wanted, as our friend
Barrow has already given us the technical part of it; which is but a
narrow contemplation of a great question sufficiently important in many
respects." Murray MS, Gifford to Murray, [September 1823]: ". . . The
Provost, from whom I heard today, promises to be ready in three or four
weeks, but wishes for a later place. He will take pains." Copleston 347

681. Article 7. Burnet's Own Times

SOUTHEY, ROBERT. Murray Reg. Murray MS, Gifford to Murray, Ramsgate, [July 1823]: "Has Southey sent anything? His last is prolix. . ."
British Museum MS, Southey to Peachey, Oct 4, 1823: "You will see in
the last Quarterly a paper of mine upon the new edition of Burnet. . ."
Cottle 242-43. Southey 577. *See also* Warter III, 398, 402, 405; Southey
416; *QR* CCX, 760

682. Article 8. Tooke on High and Low Prices

MALTHUS, THOMAS ROBERT. Murray Reg. Bonar 285, 290, 292 note
1. *D N B*

683. Article 9. Quin's Visit to Spain

WHITE, JOSEPH BLANCO. Murray Reg. British Museum MS, Southey
to Peachey, Oct 4, 1823: "You will see in the last Quarterly . . . a most
excellent [paper] . . . upon Spain by my friend Blanco White . . ." Thom
III, 468. Warter III, 405. Southey 416. Knight II, 214. *See also* Smiles
II, 57-58 and note
SOUTHEY, ROBERT. *Gentleman's* XXI, 579. *See also* Smiles II, 110

Volume XXIX, Number 58 (July 1823)
Published in December: Murray Reg.

684. Article 1. Cardinal Maury and Edward Irving's Pulpit Eloquence

MILMAN, HENRY HART. Murray Reg. Murray MS, Gifford to Murray,
[September 1823]: "Milman's promised paper, if well written, may be
serviceable—but it required considerable talent & discrimination. However, I see no reason to fear him." *See also* North in *Blackwood's* XV,
83-84

685. Article 2. Legal Oratory of Greece: Demosthenes, ed. by Planche

MITCHELL, THOMAS. Murray Reg. North in *Blackwood's* XV, 84: "the
translator of Aristophanes." *See also DNB*

686. Article 3. Faux's Memorable Days in America

BARROW, JOHN, and GIFFORD, WILLIAM. Murray Reg.: "J Barrow."
Clark 184 ("It has . . . many marks of the editor's [Gifford's] work.")
and 187: by Barrow. *See also* Smiles II, 157; North in *Blackwood's* XV, 84

687. Article 4. Lord John Russell's Don Carlos, a Tragedy

TAYLOR, HENRY, and GIFFORD, WILLIAM. Murray Reg.: "H Taylor junr & Wm Gifford." Cites unspecified old letters. Taylor I, 51 and
note, suggests only Taylor. North in *Blackwood's* XV, 85: "Gifford . . .
we think." Graham 41: Taylor. *DNB*: Taylor
CROKER, JOHN WILSON. *Gentleman's* XXI, 579

688. Article 5. Malcolm's Central India

BARROW, JOHN. Murray Reg. North in *Blackwood's* XV, 84: "every
way worthy of Mr Barrow."

689. Article 6. French Comedy

CHENEVIX, RICHARD. Murray Reg. Murray MS, Gifford to Murray,
[September 1823]: "Chenevix I thought of putting into one Art. but the
first part [see Entry 676], at all events, may be set up." North in *Blackwood's* XV, 84

690. Article 7. Superstition and Knowledge

COHEN, FRANCIS (later PALGRAVE). Murray Reg.: "Fr Palgrave."
Murray MS, Gifford to Murray, Ramsgate, [July 1823]: "Cohen must have
mistaken me or I him . . . I never thought of opening with his Art. nor
is it proper for it. I have read it this evening, & have many doubts about
its tendency:—it must, at all events, be carefully pruned. It is clever but
rash. ... Cohen wishes to have back his paper; I have therefore put it
up for him, I must beg you to give it to him." Palgrave
SOUTHEY, ROBERT. North in *Blackwood's* XV, 85: "probably Southey's."
See, however, Warter III, 427: nothing by Southey in this number of *QR*

691. Article 8. Negroes in our Colonies by Wilberforce, etc.

LOW, DAVID. Murray Reg.: "—— Low."

692. Article 9. Bornou by Capt John Adams

BARROW, JOHN. Murray Reg. North in *Blackwood's* XV, 84: "every
way worthy of Mr Barrow." *Gentleman's* XXI, 579

693. Article 10. Ecclesiastical Revenues: Francis Thackeray and A. Campbell

EDWARDS, EDWARD. Murray Reg.: "Rev E Edwards."
SOUTHEY, ROBERT. *Gentleman's* XXI, 579. *See,* however, Warter III,
427: nothing by Southey in this number of *QR*

694. Article 11. Savary, and others on the Duke d'Enghien

CROKER, JOHN WILSON. Murray Reg. Brewer MS, Murray to [Croker], [pencil notation: June 1823]: "You received I hope the Relation of Count Savary." Murray MS, Gifford to Murray, [August 1823]: "You forget to tell me the name of the French work on which you wish to set Mr Croker." North in *Blackwood's* XV, 85. Brightfield 455

Volume XXX, Number 59 (October 1823)

Published in April 1824: Murray Reg. Edited in part by Croker, Barrow, and Murray: Brightfield 182

695. Article 1. Dwight's Travels in New England

SOUTHEY, ROBERT. Murray Reg. British Museum MS, Southey to Peachey, Oct 4, 1823: "I have now begun an article upon Dr Dwight's Travels in New England & New York." Cottle 242-43. Southey 577. Warter III, 417 (one offensive alteration by Gifford), and III, 427. Graham 10. Clark 180-81 and 184: "most probably Southey's." *See also* Warter III, 341, 405-6; Southey 415

696. Article 2. Rose's Orlando Furioso

BLUNT, JOHN JAMES. Murray Reg.: "Rev T J [or J J?] Blunt."

697. Article 3. Recollections of the Peninsula by Capt Batty

PROCTER, GEORGE. Murray Reg.: "Captain Procter."

698. Article 4. Belsham's Translation of St Paul's Epistle

ROSE, HUGH JAMES. Murray Reg. Murray MS, Gifford to Murray, Ramsgate, [August 1823]: "Mr Roses address is /Revd H Rose / Horsham / Sussex." Murray MS, Gifford to Murray, [September 1823]: "I am glad you have sent Belsham to Rose. I have not seen it, in slips."
GOODHUGH, WILLIAM. *Gentleman's* XXI, 579

699. Article 5. Brooke's Travels to the North Cape

BARROW, JOHN. Murray Reg.

700. Article 6. Malaria: Blane, Koreff, Fodéré, and Julia

DUNGLISSON, ROBLEY. Murray Reg.: "Robley Dunglison." Murray MS, Gifford to Murray, [May 1824]: "There was no need to trouble Barrow with Blane's perseverance, unless he remained unsatisfied, however, tis as well as now the letter is gone."

701. Article 7. Mexico: W D Robinson, Juarros, et al

JACOB, WILLIAM. Murray Reg.: "W Jacob."

702. Article 8. Private Correspondence of Cowper

POTTER, JOHN PHILIPS. Murray Reg.: "a friend of Mr Senior, Rev. Potter."
HEBER, REGINALD. Murray MS, Gifford to Murray, Ramsgate, [July, 1823]: "I desired the Bishop of Calcutta to leave his fragments with you—has he done it? I fear not, as you do not mention it." *Gentleman's* XXI, 579, implies Heber's authorship. Graham 41

703. Article 9. Adventures of Hajji Baba

PROCTER, GEORGE. Murray Reg.: "Capt Procter."

704. Article 10. John Burridge on Naval Dry Rot

BARROW, JOHN. Murray Reg. Smiles I, 284. *Gentleman's* XXI, 579

705. Article 11. Parry's Second Voyage of Discovery, Northwest Passage

BARROW, JOHN. Murray Reg. *Gentleman's* XXI, 579

706. Article 12. Court of Chancery

CROKER, JOHN WILSON, and WRIGHT, WILLIAM. Murray Reg.:
"J W Croker." Cites unspecified old letters. Addit. note: "with valuable
information from Mr Wright a barrister." Brightfield 455: Croker

Volume XXX, Number 60 (January 1824)
Published in August: Murray Reg. Edited in part by Croker, Barrow, and
Murray: Brightfield 182

707. Article 1. McCulloch's Political Economy

MALTHUS, THOMAS ROBERT. Murray Reg. Bonar 212 note 2. Ricardo-
Malthus 179 note. *DNB. See also* Levy 374, note 177f

708. Article 2. Meyrick on Ancient Armor

PROCTER, GEORGE. Murray Reg.: "Capt Procter"

709. Article 3. White's History of Voyage to the China Sea

BARROW, JOHN. Murray Reg.

710. Article 4. Dupin's Commercial Power of England

BARROW, JOHN. Murray Reg.

711. Article 5. Smyth's Sicily

BLUNT, JOHN JAMES. Murray Reg.: "Rev J J Blunt." Murray MS,
Gifford to Murray, [May 1824]: "I . . . shall be glad to have the proof
forwarded to Mr Blunt."

712. Article 6. Prisons and Penitentiaries

TAYLOR, GEORGE. Surtees xiv
COLERIDGE, JOHN TAYLOR. Murray Reg. Murray MS, Gifford to
Murray, postmarked Ramsgate, July 22, 1824: "Mr C is too long, & I
am sorry for it. I will go to work upon it immediately, & he must see it
again, if he happens then to be in town . . . we can only wait till Mr C's
Art is ready for press. . ." Mr C may be Croker: see Entry 717

713. Article 7. Chili, Peru, etc: Schmidtmeyer, Maria Graham, and Hall

JACOB, WILLIAM. Murray Reg.: "Wm Jacob." Murray MS, Gifford to
Murray, [July 1824]: "By way of saving time I send a few pages of
America—let them be revised as soon as possible, & then put into Mr C
[pencil notation on letter says: "Coleridge?"] hands as I should wish him
to have the final view. This critique is very amusing. I am sorry it is so
long." Though J. T. Coleridge was soon to take over the editorship of
QR, "Mr C" in that letter may allude to Croker, who for some time had
assisted in editing.

714. Article 8. Hone—Aspersions Answered

ROSE, HUGH JAMES. Murray Reg.: "Rev H J Rose."

715. Article 9. Mengin's Modern Egypt

    BARROW, JOHN. Murray Reg.

716. Article 10. Landor's Imaginary Conversations

    TAYLOR, HENRY, and GIFFORD, WILLIAM. Murray Reg.: "H Taylor junr (Col. office)." Murray MS, Gifford to Murray, postmarked Ramsgate, July 22, 1824: "Let Mr Taylor have a copy of the Revise by all means—but if he has any thing to say he must be brief & quick. . . I hope he will think I have improved it. He is a nice young man, & should be encouraged." Taylor I, 79. Southey 430: parts struck out by Gifford. Graham 41: Taylor. Clark 235: Taylor

717. Article 11. Paulding's Sketch of Old England

    CROKER, JOHN WILSON, and GIFFORD, WILLIAM. Murray Reg.: "J W Croker." Murray MS, Gifford to Murray, postmarked Ramsgate, July 22, 1824: "Mr C is too long, & I am sorry for it. I will go to work upon it immediately, & he must see it again, if he happens then to be in town . . . we can only wait till Mr C's Art is ready for press . . ." This *Mr C* may be Croker, or may be Coleridge: see Entry 713. Murray MS, Gifford to Murray, postmarked Ramsgate, July 31, 1824: I return part of Paulding. Looking again at the book, I have added now & then a word. Let Croker see the whole for good and all. Murray MS, Gifford to Murray, [August 1824]: "I sent by yesterday's post Mr Croker's revise, with my own remarks—till I get it back, I cannot finish the enclosed for press; ——it is only the last leaf that I want again. Do not trouble our friend with the Revise till I have gone thro it, and then he must look at it for good and all." Murray MS, Gifford to Murray, [August 1824]: "I put in Mr C revise, a most ridiculous passage that struck me in Paulding. I care nothing about its appearance, and if it occasions any delay throw it into the fire,—as, indeed, I desired Mr C to do." Murray MS, Gifford to Murray, [August 1824]: "All that I do this morning is to return Mr C's revise for press. I have added a bit of note—but if room cannot be found for it without trouble, let it alone. It was lucky you sent on the book, for I had misunderstood two or three of Mr C's quotations—for want of some leading word. Our friend is well pleased and indeed I think his Art lively and amusing—and it is certainly useful. [¶] It can do no harm to forward a copy of the revise to Mr Ellis—I can go on with mine again— & if anything comes in time so much the better. . ." Brightfield 455: Croker

718. Article 12. Correspondence of Lady Suffolk

    SCOTT, WALTER. Murray Reg. Murray MS, Gifford to Murray, postmarked Ramsgate, August 9, 1824: ". . . I expected every day Scott's Art which did not reach me till yesterday's post . . . a clever, sensible thing; very good in the view which he takes—but perhaps not so agreeable as a more popular & more light review might have proved—tis however the work of a man who knows what he is about. Little or nothing can be done to it, on acct of its compact & dry manner—as indeed I know my friend to be so sore that I am not sorry to have so little to do. . . two [sheets] will have the extracts if any be given, which Scott has given little or no opening for, and may not perhaps much approve, when inserted." Murray MS, Gifford to Murray, postmarked Ramsgate, August 10, 1824: "I have sent . . . the remaining slips of the Suffolk Letters, with several papers marked for extracts . . . When they are printed, let Mr Croker see them, and add or diminish or take the whole away, at his pleasure. . . . it is impossible to say which Scott would have chosen. I think I have fetched up on the least objectionable, & at the same time, given a variety of styles . . . let Mr C decide . . . There is much in the Art. to be praised." Murray MS, Gifford to Murray, [August 1824]: "I see from our friends letter [perhaps Croker's] that he is very desirous of Sir Walter's appearance . . . Let it follow Paulding, for it seems that Mr C does not mean to let Sir

Walter see it again." Murray MS, Gifford to Murray, [August 1824]:
". . . who would have thought of Scott & other delays?" Smiles II, 159,
Scott. *Gentleman's* XXI, 579. Douglas II, 186, 213-14 and note. Clark
232. Brightfield 291 and note

719. Article 13. West India Colonies

HORTON, ROBERT JOHN WILMOT, and ? ELLIS, CHARLES ROSE.
Murray Reg.: "R W Horton." Murray MS, Gifford to Murray, postmarked Ramsgate, July 22, 1824: ". . . I return *by the coach* the Revise of
the West Indies, for which we are greatly obliged to my kind friend.
Pray send it to Rowarth immediately & let it be corrected without loss of
time. Let me have 2 copies, for what I have by me is so scratched and
bedevilled that the mother who bore it, would not know it. Mr Ws ['or
Mr H's' inserted above line: i.e., Wilmot, Horton, or Wilmot-Horton]
revise is not worth a single farthing. I think the paper will be important."
Murray MS, Gifford to Murray, postmarked Ramsgate, Aug 2, 1824: "I
have also put up the West India paper. Let me have a revise or rather
two copies as soon as you can, for it must be looked at again. . ." Murray
MS, Gifford to Murray, postmarked Ramsgate, August 10, 1824: "I shall
send the West Indies this week. If Mr E [letter not clear] comes, so
much the better; but we need not wait." Murray MS, Gifford to Murray,
[August 1824]: "It can do no harm to forward a copy of the revise [this
may refer to Entry 712] to Mr Ellis—I can go on with mine again—&
if anything comes in time so much the better—Where Mr Wilmot is I do
not know." Murray MS, Gifford to Murray, [August 1824]: "I enclose
Wilmot, which is a sound & useful paper—Thanks in the first place to
our good friend C. E. I think Wilmot cannot have much to do to it. . ."
Murray MS, Gifford to Murray, Ramsgate, Sunday, [August 1823]: "I
. . . now only wait for Mr Wilmot, who I hope will not meddle with what
is done; but content himself with additions—if he has anything important
to say."

Volume XXXI, Number 61 (April 1824)

Published in December: Murray Reg. Edited in part by Croker, Barrow, and
Murray: Brightfield 182

720. Article 1. Travels in Brazil: Maria Graham, Von Spix, and Von Martius

JACOB, WILLIAM. Murray Reg.: "Wm Jacob."

721. Article 2. Memoirs of Thomas Scott and John Newton

POTTER, JOHN PHILIPS. Murray Reg.: "Rev Potter"
? HEBER, REGINALD. *Gentleman's* XXI, 579

722. Article 3. Cruise's New Zealand

BARROW, JOHN. Murray Reg.

723. Article 4. Joanna Queen of Naples

PROCTER, GEORGE. Murray Reg.: "Capt Procter."

724. Article 5. Hunter and Buchanan on North American Indians

PROCTER, GEORGE. Murray Reg.: "Capt Procter." Murray Ms, Gifford
to Murray, [October 1824]: "Be so good as to send the inclosed to Mr
Procter by the quickest mode, as I have not the book, & do not know
if the names be correct . . . Beg him to return it as soon as he can, &
he shall hear from me."

725. Article 6. Biddulph's Operation of the Holy Spirit

TURTON, THOMAS. Murray Reg.: "Rev Dr Turton."

726. Article 7. Savings Banks and Country Banks

TAYLOR, GEORGE. Wales MS, Southey to Wynn, February 11, 1826: ". . . Gifford . . . admitted . . . a very able paper [on provincial currency] . . . by George Taylor . . . in the 61st number." Southey 429. Surtees xiv

727. Article 8. Lyall's Character of the Russians

BARROW, JOHN. Murray Reg.: "J Barrow." Addit. note: "See Mr Lyall's letters Feb 1825."

728. Article 9. Mitford's Village Sketches

PROCTER, GEORGE. Murray Reg.: "Capt Procter." Graham 41
? GIFFORD, WILLIAM. Hill 119: seems to imply Gifford

729. Article 10. Tour of Germany

BLUNT, JOHN JAMES. Murray Reg.

730. Article 11. Dale's Tragedies of Sophocles

HUGHES, THOMAS. Murray Reg.: "Canon Hughes."

731. Article 12. Angerstein's Collection of Pictures

ELLIS, GEORGE JAMES WELBORE AGAR (BARON DOVER). Murray Reg.: "Hon Agar Ellis."

732. Article 13. Cochrane's Pedestrian Journey in Russia and China

BARROW, JOHN. Murray Reg.

733. Article 14. New Churches. Progress of Dissent: W Newman

MILMAN, HENRY HART. Murray Reg.: "Rev H H Milman." Murray MS, Gifford to Murray, [December 24, 1824]: "I will just look at Milman, & if you will have the goodness to send your man here in *about half* an hour, he shall bring it you for press." Murray MS, Gifford to Murray, [December 24, 1824]: "You will still have, I suspect a crow to pick with Milman—The revise that he has seen, is not my revise, at least in the page form; and I have omitted a long and what I conceive, a hazardous passage, which he probably fancies not a little. I was, at first, surprised at this unusual praise—till I saw *his* revise. I know I am right."
SOUTHEY, ROBERT. Southey 577. *Gentleman's* XXI, 579. *See,* however, Warter III, 467: Southey to N. White, January 17, 1825: "The paper in the 'Quarterly' is not mine, nor have I any thing in that number."

ARTICLES WITH AUTHORS TOTALLY UNIDENTIFIED

SERIAL NUMBER	VOLUME	NUMBER	YEAR	ARTICLE	TITLE
34	I	2	1809	16	Parliamentary Reform
44	II	3	1809	9	Pinckney's Travels through France
52	II	4	1809	6	Wyvill on Intolerance
79	III	5	1810	13	French Embassy to Persia
109	IV	7	1810	8	Memoirs of Huet
120	IV	8	1810	6	Price on the Picturesque
122	IV	8	1810	8	Woodhouse's Trigonometry
130	V	9	1811	1	Clavier's Histoire . . . de la Grèce
152	V	10	1811	12	Baron Von Sach's Voyage to Surinam
205	VII	14	1812	15	W. R. Spencer's Poems
221	VIII	16	1812	1	East India Company's Charter
225	VIII	16	1812	5	Mant's Bampton Lectures
253	IX	18	1813	9	Hutton's Mathematical and Philosophical Tracts
256	IX	18	1813	12	Villani's Istorie Fiorentine
268	X	19	1813	9	Bread, Bulls, and the Inquisition
280	X	20	1814	9	Resolutions of the London Ship Owners
292	XI	21	1814	10	Kirwan's Sermons
293	XI	21	1814	11	Lacretelle's Histoire de France
295	XI	21	1814	13	History of the Azores
327	XII	24	1815	6	Cunningham's Velvet Cushion
336	XIII	25	1815	5	New Covering to a Velvet Cushion
339	XIII	25	1815	8	Gall and Spurzheim's Physiognomy
341	XIII	25	1815	10	Routh's Reliquiae Sacrae
414	XVI	32	1817	5	Miss Porden's Veils: a Poem
415	XVI	32	1817	6	Lord Amherst's Embassy—Chinese Drama

416	XVI	32	1817	7	Repton on Landscape Gardening
422	XVII	33	1817	3	Raffles's History of Java
423	XVII	33	1817	4	Miss Edgeworth's Comic Dramas
424	XVII	33	1817	5	East India College
433	XVII	34	1817	3	Hofer and the Tyrol
442	XVIII	35	1817	2	Wilks's Sketch of the South of India
443	XVIII	35	1817	3	Lives of Haydn and Mozart
445	XVIII	35	1817	5	Bentham's Plan of Parliamentary Reform
447	XVIII	35	1817	7	Adams on Cataract
448	XVIII	35	1817	8	Savigny's Naufrage de la Méduse
450	XVIII	35	1817	10	Kendall's Appeal of Murder and Trial by Battle
455	XVIII	36	1818	2	Basil Hall's Account of the Loo-choo Islands
484	XIX	38	1818	6	Sir R. Phillips on the Universe
485	XIX	38	1818	7	Brown's Northern Courts
586	XXV	49	1821	10	Scudamore on Mineral Waters
613	XXVI	52	1822	2	Bishop of St. David's Vindication of St. John
617	XXVI	52	1822	6	Arrowsmith on Instructing Deaf and Dumb
619	XXVI	52	1822	8	Harmon's Journal of Voyages . . . Western Caledonia
620	XXVI	52	1822	9	Weights and Measures
622	XXVI	52	1822	11	Ker Porter's Travels in Georgia and Persia
624	XXVI	52	1822	13	Dugald Stewart's Second Dissertation
626	XXVI	52	1822	15	Colonial Policy
629	XXVII	53	1822	3	Tour of North America: Harris, Welby, & Flower
630	XXVII	53	1822	4	Evans's Van Diemen's Land
633	XXVII	53	1822	7	Nazaroff's Expedition to Kokania
634	XXVII	53	1822	8	Montlosier: De la Monarchie Française
636	XXVII	53	1822	10	Waddington's Visit to Ethiopia
642	XXVII	54	1822	5	Jeremy Bentham's Art of Packing Juries
645	XXVII	54	1822	8	Mayow's Sermons and Miscellanies
646	XXVII	54	1822	9	Buckland on Fossil Bones
655	XXVIII	55	1822	7	Whately's Party Feeling in Matters of Religion
658	XXVIII	55	1822	10	Adultery—Prize Essay

BIBLIOGRAPHY
INDEX OF CONTRIBUTORS

BIBLIOGRAPHY WITH KEY ABBREVIATIONS

ALLIBONE   Allibone, Samuel Austin. *Critical Dictionary of English Literature.* 5 vols. Philadelphia, Lippincott, 1870

ANTHONY   Anthony, Katharine. *The Lambs, a Story of Pre-Victorian England.* New York, Knopf, 1945

BALL   Ball, Margaret. *Sir Walter Scott as a Critic of Literature.* New York, Columbia University Press, 1907. (List of 18 articles prior to 1826)

BARROW   Barrow, Sir John. *Autobiographical Memoir.* London, Murray, 1847

BEDFORD   Roberts, Barré C. *Letters and Miscellaneous Papers* [edited by G. C. Bedford] London, Bulmer, 1814

BLOMFIELD   Blomfield, Alfred. *A Memoir of Charles James Blomfield, with Selections from His Correspondence.* 2 vols. London, Murray, 1863

BONAR   Bonar, James. *Malthus and His Work.* New York, Macmillan, 1924

BONNELL   Bonnell, Henry H. *Charlotte Brontë, George Eliot, Jane Austen: Studies in Their Work.* New York, Longmans, 1902

BOWLES   Southey, Robert. *Correspondence of Robert Southey with Caroline Bowles,* edited by Edward Dowden. Dublin, Hodges, 1881

BRANDE   Brande's *Quarterly Journal of Science,* XXVIII (1829), 154-60. (Thomas Young's own list of his contributions to *QR*)

BREWER MS   The Brewer Collection at the Library of the University of Iowa, Iowa City, Iowa. This collection includes about 300 letters that passed between members of *The Quarterly Review* group. Most of them are from John Murray II to John Wilson Croker; a few are from William Gifford to John Murray II. Some of the letters were dated when written; a few bear later pencil notations concerning dates; but many of the dates can be only approximated. Professor Andrew J. Green's careful typescripts, which are included in the collection, furnish the approximations that he was able to arrive at through the use of watermarks and various allusions within the letters. But presumably the evidence of handwriting itself has not been exploited. Some manuscripts written apparently close together in time and signed with Murray's name seem much less uniform in handwriting than others written apparently in different decades. The most exceptional example of that difference, Letter 66, furnished us only one note: *see* Entry 396

BRIGHTFIELD Brightfield, Myron F. *John Wilson Croker.* Berkeley, California, University of California Press, 1940. (List of Croker's contributions to *QR*)

BRITISH MUSEUM MS Two collections of Southey MS letters at the British Museum, London, England. 1) The collection of Southey's letters to General William Peachey (B.M. Addit. MS 28603) includes some 50 dated letters written between 1808 and 1837. 2) The collection of Southey's letters to Charles Danvers (B.M. Addit. MS 30928) includes some 75 dated letters written between 1799 and 1813. Both those collections have been photographed on microfilm by the Modern Language Association of America. And the M.L.A. films (821 F and 822 F), now deposited at the Library of Congress, Washington, D. C., are available on interlibrary loan

BROUGHTON Broughton, Lord (John Cam Hobhouse). *Recollections of a Long Life, with Additional Extracts from His Private Diaries,* edited by His Daughter Lady Dorchester. 6 vols. London, Murray, 1909

BUTLER Butler, H. J., and Butler, H. E. "Sir Walter Scott and Maria Edgeworth: Some Unpublished Letters." *Modern Language Review,* XXIII (1928), 273-98

BYRON Byron, Lord (George Gordon Byron). *Lord Byron's Correspondence, Chiefly with Lady Melbourne, Mr Hobhouse, the Hon. Douglas Kinnard, and P. B. Shelley,* edited by John Murray. 2 vols. London, Murray, 1922

CAIRNS I Cairns, William B. *British Criticism of American Writings, 1783-1815.* Madison, Wisconsin, 1918. (University of Wisconsin Studies in Language and Literature, No. 1)

CAIRNS II Cairns, William B. *British Criticism of American Writings, 1815-1833.* Madison, Wisconsin, 1922. (University of Wisconsin Studies in Language and Literature, No. 14)

CANONGATE Scott, Sir Walter. *Chronicles of the Canongate.* 2 vols. Edinburgh, Cadell, 1827. (28 pp. Introduction signed by Walter Scott, Abbotsford, October 1, 1827)

CLARK Clark, Roy Benjamin. *William Gifford, Tory Satirist, Critic and Editor.* New York, Columbia University Press, 1930

COLERIDGE Coleridge, Lord (Bernard John Seymour Coleridge). *Story of a Devonshire House.* London, Unwin, 1905

COOK Cook, Davidson. "Murray's Mysterious Contributor." *Nineteenth Century,* CI (April 1927), 605-13

COOKE'S MEM. Robert Cooke's Memorandum Book of John Murray. *See* under *Murray Reg.* in this Bibliography

COPLESTON Copleston, William James. *Memoir of Edward Copleston, Bishop of Llandaff, with Selections from His Diary and Correspondence.* London, Parker, 1851

CORSON Corson, James Clarkson. *A Bibliography of Sir Walter Scott, a Classified and Annotated List of Books and Articles . . . 1797-1940.* Edinburgh, Oliver, 1943

COTTLE — Cottle, Joseph. *Reminiscences of Samuel Taylor Coleridge and Robert Southey.* London, Haulston, 1848

CROKER — Croker, John Wilson. *Essays on the Early Period of the French Revolution. Reprinted from "The Quarterly Review," with Additions and Corrections.* London, Murray, 1857

CUNNINGHAM — Cunningham, Allan. *Biographical and Critical History of the British Literature of the Last Fifty Years.* Paris, 1834

DAVISON — Davison, John. *Remarks on Baptismal Regeneration.* Oxford, Parker, 1847. *British Museum Catalogue:* From the *Quarterly Review,* July, 1810 [i.e. 1816?]

DOUGLAS — Scott, Sir Walter. *Familiar Letters,* edited by David Douglas. 2 vols. Boston, Houghton, 1894

D'OYLY — D'Oyly, George. *Sermons, With a Memoir by His Son* [C. J. D'Oyly]. 2 vols. London, Rivington, 1847

DUDLEY — Dudley, Lord (John William Ward). *Letters of the Earl of Dudley to the Bishop of Llandaff,* edited by Edward Copleston, Bishop of Llandaff. London, Murray, 1840

DUDLEY-IVY — Dudley, Lord (John William Ward). *Letters to "Ivy" from the First Earl of Dudley,* edited by S. H. Romilly. New York, Longmans, 1905

EDGEWORTH — Edgeworth, Maria. *The Life and Letters of Maria Edgeworth,* edited by Augustus J. C. Hare. 2 vols. Boston, Houghton, 1895

EICHLER — Eichler, Albert. *John Hookham Frere.* Vienna, Braumüller, 1905

FITZPATRICK — Fitzpatrick, William John. *Lady Morgan: Her Career, Literary and Personal.* London, Skeet, 1860

FITZPATRICK'S *Whately* — Fitzpatrick, William John. *Memoirs of Richard Whately, Archbishop of Dublin, with a Glance at His Contemporaries and Times.* 2 vols. London, Bentley, 1864

FORSTER — Forster, John. *Walter Savage Landor.* Boston, Fields, 1869

FRERE — Frere, John Hookham. *Works, with a Prefatory Memoir,* edited by Sir Bartle Frere; 2d revised edition. 3 vols. London, Pickering, 1874

FYFE — Fyfe, W. T. *Edinburgh Under Sir Walter Scott,* with an Introduction by R. S. Rait. New York, Dutton, 1907

Gentleman's — *Gentleman's Magazine,* XXI (1844), 137-41, 577-80; XXVIII (1847), pt. 2, 34-37. (List of contributors to *QR,* Vols. I-XXXIX)

GRAHAM — Graham, Walter. *Tory Criticism in The Quarterly Review, 1809-1853.* New York, Columbia University Press, 1921

GRAHAM IN *MLN* — Graham, Walter. "Scott's Dilemma." *Modern Language Notes,* XLI (1926), 45-47

GRAHAM IN *PMLA* — Graham, Walter. "Contemporary Critics of Coleridge." *Publications of the Modern Language Association,* XXXVIII (1923), 278-89

GRAHAM IN *PQ* — Graham, Walter. "Robert Southey as Tory Reviewer." *Philological Quarterly,* II (1923), 97-111

GRAHAM IN *SP* — Graham, Walter. "Some Infamous Tory Reviews." *Studies in Philology,* XXII (1925), 500-17

GREEVER   Greever, Garland. *A Wiltshire Parson*. London, Constable
                 [1926]

GREVILLE   Greville, Charles Cavendish Fulke. *The Greville Memoirs,*
                 1814-1860, edited by Giles Lytton Strachey and Roger Ful-
                 ford. 8 vols. London, Macmillan, 1938

GRIERSON   Scott, Sir Walter. *Letters,* edited by Sir H. J. C. Grierson.
                 12 vols. London, Constable, 1932-37

GRIERSON'S   Grierson, Sir H. J. C. *Sir Walter Scott, Bart.* New York,
  Scott   Columbia University Press, 1938

GRIGGS   Coleridge, Samuel Taylor. *Unpublished Letters,* edited by
                 Earl Leslie Griggs. 2 vols. London, Constable, 1932

HALLER   Haller, William. "Southey's Later Radicalism." *Publications*
                 of the Modern Language Association, XXXVII (1922),
                 281-92

HAMMOND   George Hammond's marked *Quarterly Review,* at Maryville
                 College Library, Maryville, Tennessee. On the Table of
                 Contents of Hammond's copy of *QR* No. 2, someone has
                 written in pencil the names of four authors. Parts of the
                 names have been cut away by the binder. Hammond, first
                 British Minister to the United States, was a member of the
                 group that founded *The Quarterly Review*

HAZLITT   Hazlitt, William. *The Spirit of the Age. To Which is Added*
                 "Free Thoughts on Public Affairs" and *"A Letter to Wil-*
                 liam Gifford." 4th edition. London, Bell, 1894

HEBER   Heber, Mrs Amelia Shipley. *The Life of Reginald Heber,*
                 Lord Bishop of Calcutta. 2 vols. New York, Protestant
                 Episcopal Press, 1830

HILDYARD   Hildyard, M. C. "John Gibson Lockhart." *Cornhill Maga-*
                 zine, LXXII (1932), 371-82

HILL   Hill, Constance. *Mary Russell Mitford and Her Surround-*
                 ings. London, Lane, 1920

HILLHOUSE   Hillhouse, J. T. *The Waverley Novels and Their Critics.*
                 Minneapolis, University of Minnesota Press, 1936

HOGAN   Hogan, Charles Beecher. "Sir Walter Scott and *Emma*"
                 Publications of the Modern Language Association, XLV
                 (1930), 1264-66

HOLLOWAY   Holloway, Owen E. "George Ellis, *The Anti-Jacobin* and
                 The Quarterly Review." *Review of English Studies,* X
                 (1934) 55-66

HOPPNER   McKay, William, and Roberts, W. *John Hoppner, R. A.* Lon-
                 don, Bell, 1909

HORNER   Horner, Francis. *Memoirs and Correspondence,* edited by
                 Leonard Horner. 2 vols. London, Murray, 1843

HUCHON   Huchon, René. *George Crabbe and His Times, 1754-1832,*
                 translated by Frederick Clarke. London, Murray, 1907

HUTCHINSON   Lamb, Charles. *Works,* edited by Thomas Hutchinson; Ox-
                 ford edition. Vol. 1. London, Humphrey Milford [1908]

IDMAN   Idman, Niilo. *Charles Robert Maturin*. London, Constable,
                 1923

JENNINGS   Croker, John Wilson. *The Correspondence and Diaries,* edited
                 by L. J. Jennings. 2 vols. New York, Scribners, 1884

JERDAN   Jerdan, William. *The autobiography of William Jerdan with His Literary, Political and Social Reminiscences and Correspondence during the Last Fifty Years.* 4 vols. London, Hall, 1852-53

KERN   Kern, J. D. "An Unidentified Review, Possibly by Scott." *Modern Language Quarterly,* VI (1945), 327-28

KERN AND SCHNEIDER   Kern, J. D.; Schneider, E.; and Griggs, Irwin. "Lockhart to Croker on the *Quarterly.*" *Publications of the Modern Language Association,* LX (1945), 175-98

KEYNES   Keynes, Geoffrey. *Jane Austen, a Bibliography.* London, Nonesuch Press, 1929

KNIGHT   Knight, William, ed. *Memorials of Coleorton: Being Letters from Coleridge, Wordsworth and His Sister, Southey and Sir Walter Scott, to Sir George and Lady Beaumont of Coleorton, Leicestershire, 1803 to 1834.* 2 vols. Edinburgh, Douglas, 1887

KNIGHT *Letters*   Knight, William, ed. *Letters of the Wordsworth Family, from 1787 to 1855.* 3 vols. Boston, Ginn, 1907

KUNITZ   Kunitz, Stanley J., ed. *British Authors of the Nineteenth Century.* New York, Wilson, 1936

LAMB   Lamb, Charles. *The Works of Charles and Mary Lamb,* edited by E. V. Lucas. 7 vols. London, Methuen, 1903-05

LAMBERT   Lambert, Mildred, and Hillhouse, J. T. "The Scott Letters in the Huntington Library." *Huntington Library Quarterly,* II (1939) 319-52

LANG   Lang, Andrew. "Scott His Own Reviewer." *The Sketch,* VIII (Dec. 5, 1894), Supplement, p. 2

LEVY   Levy, S. Leon. *Nassau W. Senior, the Prophet of Modern Capitalism.* Boston, Humphries, c. 1943

LOCKHART   Lockhart, John Gibson. *Memoirs of the Life of Sir Walter Scott, Bart.,* new edition. 9 vols. Boston, Ticknor, 1861-64

LUCAS   Lamb, Charles. *The Letters of Charles Lamb, to Which Are Added Those of His Sister Mary Lamb,* edited by E. V. Lucas. 3 vols. London, Dent, 1935

MARRIOTT   Marriott, J. A. R. *George Canning and His Times.* London, Murray, 1903. (Appendix: Canning and the Quarterly Review, pp. 145-56)

MARSHALL   Marshall, Roderick. *Italy in English Literature, 1755-1815.* New York, Columbia University Press, 1934

MERIVALE   Merivale, Anna W., comp. *Family Memorials.* Exeter, Upward, 1884

MILMAN   Milman, Arthur. *Henry Hart Milman, Dean of St. Paul's.* London, Murray, 1900

MITFORD   L'Estrange, Alfred Guy, ed. *The Friendships of Mary Russell Mitford.* 2 vols. London, Hurst, 1882

MONK   Monk, Charles J. "Edinburgh Critics and Quarterly Reviewers." *The Athenaeum,* No. 2473 (March 20, 1875), p. 393-95

MOORE   Moore, Thomas. *Memoirs, Journal and Correspondence,* edited by Lord John Russell. 8 vols. London, Longmans, 1853

MORGAN MS   Southey Letters and documents at J. Pierpont Morgan Library, 29 East 36th Street, New York, New York. Most of these letters are from Southey to J. W. Croker

MORLEY
Robinson, Henry Crabbe. *The Correspondence of Henry Crabbe Robinson with the Wordsworth Circle (1808-1866); . . . from the Originals in Dr Williams's Library, London,* edited by Edith J. Morley. 2 vols. Oxford, Clarendon Press, 1927

MOZLEY
Mozeley, Thomas. *Reminiscences, Chiefly of Oriel College and the Oxford Movement.* 2 vols. Boston, Houghton, 1882

MURRAY MS
Murray MS letters at Sir John Murray's, 50 Albemarle Street, London. These MSS include over 500 letters from editor William Gifford to owner John Murray II, a few from Gifford to John Ireland, and a few from other writers. Many of the Gifford letters were hastily done notes, written without date and sent by messenger. Later hands have supplied approximate dates for most of them, and frequently supplied other helpful notations. A few letters have been annotated by John Murray II, to whom they were written

MURRAY REG.
Murray's Register of Authors and Articles in *The Quarterly Review,* at Sir John Murray's, 50 Albemarle Street, London. This list of articles and their authors, compiled apparently by John Murray IV and extending from 1809 to 1879, has obviously been revised with care. Frequently it indicates the authority upon which an attribution of authorship is based. That is, the authority may be (1) Murray II's marked file of *The Quarterly Review.* Or it may be (2) Robert Cooke's Memorandum Book of John Murray. Cooke was a nephew of John Murray II and a trusted member of the firm, at least by the late 1830's. Or finally it may be (3) files of unspecified old letters. Furthermore, blank pages opposite these formal entries sometimes contain informal Additional Notes by various hands, referring to specific letters from Gifford, George Ellis, and others. Though those Addit. Notes are not all uniformly critical, most are helpful

NAPIER
Napier, Macvey. *Selections from the Correspondence of Macvey Napier,* edited by his son, Macvey Napier. London, Macmillan, 1879

NICHOLS
[Nichols, John Gough] *Biographical Memoirs of Thomas Dunham Whitaker.* No place, no date, xliv pp.

NORTH
North, Christopher (pseud. of John Wilson). "Note on the Quarterly Reviewers." *Blackwood's Edinburgh Magazine,* XV (1824), 83-85

PALGRAVE
Palgrave, Sir Francis. *Collected Historical Works,* edited by Sir R. H. I. Palgrave. Vols IX-X. Cambridge, University Press, 1922

PASTON
Paston, George (pseud. of Emily Morse Symonds). *At John Murray's: Records of a Literary Circle 1843-1892.* New York, Dutton, 1932

PASTON
Memoirs
Paston, George (pseud. of Emily Morse Symonds). *Little Memoirs of the Eighteenth Century.* New York, Dutton, 1901

PETTIGREW
Pettigrew, Thomas Joseph. *Biographical Memoirs of the Most Celebrated Physicians, Surgeons, etc, etc,* London, Whitaker, 1840. (Vol. IV, p. 21, contains list of Young's contributions to *Q.R.*)

PFEIFFER
Pfeiffer, Karl G. "The Authorship of Certain Articles in The Quarterly Review." *Philological Quarterly,* XI (1932), 97-108. "Review of Clark's Gifford." *Philological Quarterly* XI (1932), 411-13

QR

Quarterly Review, LXVII (1840), 79-117. (Article on Lord Dudley)
Quarterly Review, CXXXII (1872), 26-59. (Article on John Hookham Frere)
Quarterly Review, CCX (1909), 731 ff. (QR's Centenary Article)

REITZEL

Reitzel, William. "Sir Walter Scott's Review of Jane Austen's Emma." Publications of the Modern Language Association, XLIII (1928), 487-93

RICARDO

Ricardo, David. Letters of David Ricardo to Thomas Robert Malthus, edited by James Bonar. Oxford, Clarendon Press, 1887

RICARDO-
TROWER

Ricardo, David. Letters of David Ricardo to Hutches Trower and Others: 1811-1823, edited by James Bonar and J. H. Hollander. Oxford, Clarendon Press, 1899

RICKMAN

Williams, Orlo. Lamb's Friend the Census-Taker. Life and Letters of John Rickman. London, Constable, 1911

ROBBERDS

Robberds, J. W., comp. and ed. A Memoir of the Life and Writings of William Taylor of Norwich. 2 vols. London, Murray, 1843

ROBINSON

Robinson, Henry Crabbe. On Books and Their Writers, edited by Edith J. Morley. 3 vols. London, Dent, 1938

ROGERS

Roberts, R. Ellis. Samuel Rogers and His Circle. London, Methuen [1910]

ROMILLY

Romilly, Sir Samuel. Memoirs of the Life of Sir Samuel Romilly, Written by Himself, with a Selection from His Correspondence, edited by his Sons; 2d ed. 3 vols. London, Murray, 1840

ROMILLY-
EDGEWORTH

Romilly, Samuel Henry, ed. Romilly-Edgeworth Letters, 1813-1818. London, Murray [1936]

ROSE

Rose, J. H. New General Biographical Dictionary. 12 vols. London, Fellowes, 1850

RUSSELL

Russell, Lord John. Early Correspondence: 1805-1840, edited by Rollo Russell. 2 vols. London, Unwin [1913]

SALT

Salt, Henry. Life and Correspondence, edited by J. J. Halls. 2 vols. London, Bentley, 1834

SCOTT

Scott, Sir Walter. The Miscellaneous Works. Vols. XVII-XXI. Edinburgh, Black, 1870-82

SCOTT-MARURIN

Scott, Sir Walter. The Correspondence of Sir Walter Scott and Charles Robert Maturin, edited by F. E. Ratchford and W. M. McCarthy. Austin, Texas, University of Texas Press, 1937

SELINCOURT

Wordsworth, William. The Letters of William and Dorothy Wordsworth; the Middle Years; arranged and edited by Ernest de Selincourt. 2 vols. Oxford, Clarendon press, 1937

SENIOR

Senior, Nassau W. Essays on Fiction. London, Longmans, 1864

SEYMOUR

Seymour, Lady, ed. The "Pope" of Holland House; Selections from the Correspondence of John Wishaw and His Friends: 1813-1840 (With a Memoir of Wishaw and an Account of "The King of Clubs," by W. P. Courtney). London, Unwin, 1906

SHARPE | Sharpe, Charles Kirkpatrick. *Letters from and to Charles Kirkpatrick Sharpe; with a Memoir by the Rev. W. K. R. Bedford.* 2 vols. Edinburgh, Blackwood, 1888

SIMMONS | Simmons, Jack. *Southey.* London, Collins, 1945

Sketches | *Sketches of Eminent Medical Men.* Philadelphia, American Sunday School Union, n.d. (Sketch of Robert Gooch and attribution of one *QR* article to him)

SMILES | Smiles, Samuel. *Memoir and Correspondence of John Murray.* 2 vols. London, Murray, 1891

SMITH | Smith, Sydney. *Essays, Social and Political; First and Second Series in one Volume.* London, Ward, n.d.

SNYDER | Snyder, Franklyn Bliss. *The Life of Robert Burns.* New York, Macmillan, 1932

SOUTHEY | Southey, Robert. *The Life and Correspondence of Robert Southey,* edited by Charles Cuthbert Southey. New York, Harper, 1851. (List of articles contributed by Southey to *QR* up to 1838)

SOUTHEY *Essays* | Southey, Robert. *Essays, Moral and Political.* 2 vols. London, Murray, 1832

SPURGEON | Spurgeon, Caroline F. E. *Five Hundred Years of Chaucer Criticism and Allusion, 1357-1900.* 3 vols. Cambridge, University Press, 1925

SURTEES | Taylor, George. *Memoir of Robert Surtees; with additions by James Raine.* Durham, Publications of the Surtees Society [1852] (List of articles contributed to *QR* by George Taylor)

TAYLOR | Taylor, Henry. *Autobiography.* 2 vols. New York, Harper, 1885

THOM | White, Blanco. *The Life of the Rev. Joseph Blanco White ... with Portions of His Correspondence,* edited by John Hamilton Thom. 3 vols. London, Chapman, 1845. (Lists White's contributions to *QR*)

TICKNOR | Ticknor, George. *Life, Letters and Journals;* 6th ed. 2 vols. Boston, Osgood, 1877

TLS | "Scott as Critic and Judge," *Times Literary Supplement,* Nov. 7, 1918, pp. 529-30

TUCKWELL | Tuckwell, W. *Pre-Tractarian Oxford.* London, Smith, 1909

WALES MS | Southey's letters to C. W. W. Wynn in the National Library of Wales, Aberystwith, Wales. Our knowledge of this collection is limited to a few relevant items that Professor Kenneth Curry of the University of Tennessee copied or digested for us

WARTER | Southey, Robert. *Selections from the Letters of Robert Southey,* edited by John Wood Warter. 4 vols. London, Longmans, 1856

WHATELY | Whately, Richard. *Miscellaneous Lectures and Reviews.* London, Parker, 1861

WHEWELL | Whewell, William. *History of the Inductive Sciences.* 3 vols. London, Parker, 1837

WHITE | White, Newman Ivey. *The Unextinguished Hearth: Shelley and His Contemporary Critics.* Durham, Duke University Press, 1938

WICKS   Wicks, Margaret C. W. *The Italian Exiles in London, 1816-1848.* Manchester, University of Manchester Press, 1937

WILBERFORCE   Wilberforce, William. *Correspondence,* edited by Robert Isaac Wilberforce and Samuel Wilberforce. 2 vols. London, Murray, 1840

WILLIAMS   Williams, E. Baumer. "Some Unpublished Letters of Robert Southey." *Blackwood's Edinburgh Magazine,* CLXIV (1898), 167-85

WORDSWORTH   Wordsworth, William. *Some Letters of the Wordsworth Family, Now First Published with a Few Unpublished Letters of Coleridge and Southey and Others,* edited by by L. N. Broughton. Ithaca, New York, Cornell University Press, 1942. (Cornell Studies in English, vol. XXXII)

YOUNG   Peacock, George. *Life of Thomas Young, M.D., F.R.S.* London, Murray, 1855

INDEX OF CONTRIBUTORS*

Under each author's name are listed the serial numbers of the articles that have been associated with him. Regular straight type indicates positive attribution; italic type indicates questionable or doubtful association. Collaboratively written articles are listed under more than one reviewer.

* For all matters other than the authors, see the elaborate general indices to *The Quarterly Review.* Those index volumes were published at intervals of ten years as uniform parts of the *QR* file. The two index volumes that cover the period of Gifford's editorship (1809 to 1825) are Vol. XX(1820) and Vol. XL(1831).